No Way Out

The Gift Of Absolute Freedom

by Charlie Hayes

ISBN 13 978-0-9766619-9-3
ISBN 0-9766619-9-3
To order additional copies, please contact:
Nonduality Expressions
1-580-366-4083
non.duality@yahoo.com

"The succession of transient moments creates the illusion of time, but the timeless reality of pure being is not in movement, for all movement requires a motionless background. It is itself the background. Once you have found it in yourself, you know that you had never lost that independent being."

- *Sri Nisargadatta Maharaj*

Contact the Author

Your comments, questions,
insights are most welcome...
e-mail: charliehayes36@yahoo.com
or phone: USA + 1-580-366-4083

Visit http://www.theeternalstate.org

http://charlesdavidhayes.blogspot.com/

http://reiki-now.blogspot.com/

http://motorsports-sponsorship.blogspot.com/

And ... See Charlie on YouTube:

http://www.youtube.com/profile?user=charlesdavidhayes

What Readers Say About Earlier Books...

On "From I Am To I Am, With Love"

"It is obvious that some have already benefited deeply and their doubts and suffering have been eased or eradicated. That is what it is all about. The message is clear and shared with great enthusiasm and love. Your words and example are making a positive impact; there is no doubt about it." - *John Wheeler*

"I certainly endorse this book." - *'Sailor' Bob Adamson*

"Charlie is not offering simply another step along the path. He invites you to end the search right here and right now." - *Burt Jurgens, beyondescription.net*

"Charlie is a born teacher. Having been a self-admitted 'tough nut to crack,' he deeply understands the pitfalls of Advaita, and knows how to help others find their way. Empathetic and yet direct, Charlie packs a powerful punch with his words. Good, clear pointing." - *Annette Nibley, whatneverchanges.com*

"Charlie Hayes has written an excellent book on that which is the basis of all that is, and that is not. This book cuts through all the advaita jargon and gives it to you in easy to understand language. there is no-one to be enlightened there is only whatever is arising in awareness. this is the end of all searching, read and let what is being pointed to resonate in understanding the egg will crack and what is there all along will be realized for no-one. Charlie thank you for giving this gift to the world." - *Marc Josef, NY*

"Charlie tells it like it is and delivers the timeless message of Advaita in the tradition of Sri Nisargadatta and Bob Adamson. From the very first pages you are given the tools to know who you are and to investigate that until there are no doubts left. I am so grateful to Charlie for creating this guide book and sharing his time and energy without which knowing that "I Am" would have been mere words. Through the efforts of people like Charlie, there is a growing movement in Advaita today that was first sprouted in India, cultivated in Australia and has now taken root here in America. If you are finally finished wondering when "you" will get it, read this book and end the search". *-Greg LeBlanc, CA*

"This wonderful book exudes love and immediate presence. If you want the feeling of actually sitting with a great teacher, but don't have access to a live teacher, this book gives you the sense Charlie is right there with you. It's much more than just reading a book." *-David Trindle, PA*

"This is a beautiful gem of a book; written by a wonderful man. Highly recommended". *-Colin Bright, U.K.*

On "Life After Death"

"I was very happy to read this new book ('Life After Death') by my dear friend, Charlie. It is chock full of pointers that direct the reader back to who they already and really are. Highly recommended!" *-Nathan Spoon, VA*

"This text - and the Energy of Love from which it arose - is pointing to something that you don't know that you don't know. What could that be? Are you living a life you love? "Life After Death is a free-wheeling spiritual romp that points directly to the Truth of who you really are. . .deep down.

The Author blasts open the doors of misperception with his very readable and entertaining style that compels the Reader to go both onward and inward.

In the end, Charlie succeeds brilliantly in his mission to dis-illusion the Reader from the long-standing belief in the existence of an individual and separate "person-hood." Highly recommended. *-Chuck Hillig, author of "Looking for God, finding the (W)hole on One"*

"Thanks so much for the book "Life After Death" ... I actually read about half of it today. Very "interesting" life.... But we both know it's all bullshit - some of the things you say about how you were not honest is very true for most of us. You paint a very lovely (and ugly) picture of a life spent seeking. In fact seeking itself becomes the problem - it is the very search itself which seemingly "prevents" seeing.... however upon investigation it is clear that even the seeking and suffering could not be known as anything outside of this awareness which you are, which I am.

"It is clear that the intelligence-energy expresses through the thought "I AM." This activity of knowing is the very ground of all experiences, good, bad and ugly. It is the basis for consciousness manifesting as this solid block of reality, this universe... This I AM was accepted without question until investigated. Your insights are very clear - you offer a sometimes gentle tug, sometimes harsh kick in the ass, to accept the invitation surrounding this "restless" mind.
"True teachers who have a clear insight have often arisen as harsh, eccentric and explosive. You seem to be the epitome of these - the "in your face" style of sharing in this simple livingness as it is, right now. You are another beautiful expression of THIS". - *Randall Friend*

"Until you are free of the drug [of self-identification], all your religions and sciences, prayers and yogas are of no use to you, for, based on a mistake, they strengthen it."

-Sri Nisargadatta Maharaj

Acknowledgments

There is a movement of thought-energy that seems to want to say "thank you" to some other not-persons who point to What Is (Nothing Being Everything) in unique and amazingly patient and unconditionally loving ways. There have been many such appearances in the dream-life of "Charlie." ... and any list will be both way too short and (since there IS no-one anywhere) ridiculously long!

Three non-persons simply must be acknowledged here, why I do not know but, well, this is what' happening: So ...

To John Wheeler ... Thanks for Being The Patience Of Job

To 'Sailor' Bob Adamson ...Thanks for Not Buying My "Poor Me" Story

To Tony Parsons ... thanks for Nothing Being Everything.

The One Ocean of Absolute Being bubbles and waves and arises as the froth on the shore but it's all still water. All these wondrous "teachers of nothing" arise from the Absolute yet are never NOT The Absolute. Nor are YOU.

But then, too many words spoil the froth.

Enjoy the book, and get in touch if Aliveness moves the happening of that.

Love,

Charlie Hayes
Enid, Oklahoma
Winter 2007-2008

Table of Contents

"You are prior to consciousness, prior to being, prior to presence, prior to the knower, prior to stillness."

- John Wheeler

"Because awareness is self existing there is no effort needed or anyone who can make an effort to get it or lose it."

- 'Sailor' Bob Adamson

"Though unknown and unknowable, my real Being is concrete and solid like a rock."

- Sri Nisargadatta Maharaj

"Being is the one and only constant that never comes and never goes away. Because it is nothing and everything it cannot be gained or lost, given or received, approached or avoided."

- Tony Parsons

"That which permeates all, which nothing transcends and which, like the universal space around us, fills everything completely from within and without, that Supreme non-dual Brahman -- that thou art."

- Adi Shankara

"The place where even the slightest trace of the 'I' does not exist, alone is Self."

- Sri Ramana Maharshi

Introduction

A Few Notes From The Unborn To The Unborn ....

A Note About "Teachers"

In this correspondence (and in my books) it may appear that there is "someone here teaching" and "someone out there learning." This is a false paradigm. I consider what happens around here to be sharing and pointing out what worked to ease, and end, my own psychological suffering, as a friend, not a teacher or a guru.

A seeker that takes himself or herself to be a separate person will always see other persons, and this almost inevitably reinforces the false sense of separateness which is the root cause of personal psychological suffering. In my view, this false personal identity cannot be seen through when the assumption is that there is a teacher who can teach "me" how to "attain" transformation, enlightenment, liberation or whatever your favorite myth-word might be. We reiterate here constantly that there is NO teacher and NO student in Truth and what happens here is, the false is pointed out AS false and the Real (Awareness-Being-ItSelf) as Real ... happening in and from Oneness ItSelf... so to say.

No-one is doing this; it is a happening of the Heart of all communing with ItSelf. Impossible to grasp and impossible to teach. Yet sharing happens. So if you take me to be a teacher and yourself to be a student, the message cannot be heard and the seeking mind will seek more and better answers ... forever!

See if that paradigm can be seen right now as a false, made-up assumption of separateness ... two-ness … and see right now that Being IS and cannot be divided. This Beingness can only APPEAR to be divided by language, the creator of the false paradigm of separateness. But the false cannot stand up to rigorous investigation.

I do not take myself to be a teacher. Please do not take me to be a teacher, and please do not take yourself to be a student. Let us simply be friends, sharing what works and looking into what IS together in The One Heart of Communication … One to One. Thank you!

I: Absolute Freedom is Unimaginable

There is simply NO way "I" could have imagined the Absolute Freedom that is "revealed" when the belief in a separate "me" dies out. Unbounded Freedom? Yes ... but for NO ONE.

The impossibility of expressing the inexpressible is, however, surprisingly NOT "frustrating" ... there is simply no "me" to be "frustrated" or not, in this Empty Fullness that simply IS. This Isness is both the most deliciously REAL and the most unimaginably Unreal. Not Two.

So this book is a rambling rosebush with both thorns and blossoms, and the sweet smell of the flower intermingles with the stench of congested thought (rather like manure, great fertilizer!) ... and so the expression happens here and this happening can neither be caused nor prevented.

II: Zen Mind is No Mind

"To this ultimate state, no law or description applies"

The Hsin-Hsin Ming

Verses on the Faith-Mind

By Seng-ts'an,
Third Chinese Patriarch
Translated by Richard B. Clarke

The Great Way is not difficult
for those not attached to preferences.
When neither love nor hate arises,
all is clear and undisguised.
Separate by the smallest amount, however,
and you are as far from it as heaven is from earth.

If you wish to know the truth,
then hold to no opinions for or against anything.
To set up what you like against what you dislike
is the disease of the mind.

When the fundamental nature of things is not recognized
the mind's essential peace is disturbed to no avail.
The Way is perfect as vast space is perfect,
where nothing is lacking and nothing is in excess.

Indeed, it is due to our grasping and rejecting
that we do not know the true nature of things.
Live neither in the entanglements of outer things,
nor in ideas or feelings of emptiness.
Be serene and at one with things
and erroneous views will disappear by themselves.

When you try to stop activity to achieve quietude,
your very effort fills you with activity.
As long as you remain attached to one extreme or another
you will never know Oneness.
Those who do not live in the Single Way
cannot be free in either activity or quietude, in assertion or denial.

Deny the reality of things
and you miss their reality;
assert the emptiness of things
and you miss their reality.
The more you talk and think about it
the further you wander from the truth.
So cease attachment to talking and thinking,
and there is nothing you will not be able to know.

To return to the root is to find the essence,
but to pursue appearances or "enlightenment" is to miss the source.
To awaken even for a moment
is to go beyond appearance and emptiness.

Changes that seem to occur in the empty world
we make real only because of our ignorance.

Do not seek for the truth;
Only cease to cherish opinions.

Do not remain in a dualistic state;
avoid such easy habits carefully.
If you attach even to a trace
of this and that, of right and wrong,
the Mind-essence will be lost in confusion.

Although all dualities arise from the One,
do not be attached even to ideas of this One.

When the mind exists undisturbed in the Way,
there is no objection to anything in the world;
and when there is no objection to anything,
things cease to be— in the old way.
When no discriminating attachment arises,
the old mind ceases to exist.
Let go of things as separate existences
and mind too vanishes.
Likewise when the thinking subject vanishes
so too do the objects created by mind.

The arising of other gives rise to self;
giving rise to self generates others.
Know these seeming two as facets
of the One Fundamental Reality.
In this Emptiness, these two are really one—
and each contains all phenomena.
If not comparing, nor attached to "refined" and "vulgar"—
you will not fall into judgment and opinion.

The Great Way is embracing and spacious—
to live in it is neither easy nor difficult.
Those who rely on limited views are fearful and irresolute:
The faster they hurry, the slower they go.
To have a narrow mind,
and to be attached to getting enlightenment
is to lose one's center and go astray.

When one is free from attachment,
all things are as they are,
and there is neither coming nor going.

When in harmony with the nature of things, your own fundamental nature,
and you will walk freely and undisturbed.
However, when mind is in bondage, the truth is hidden,
and everything is murky and unclear,
and the burdensome practice of judging
brings annoyance and weariness.
What benefit can be derived
from attachment to distinctions and separations?

If you wish to move in the One Way,
do not dislike the worlds of senses and ideas.
Indeed, to embrace them fully
is identical with true Enlightenment.
The wise person attaches to no goals
but the foolish person fetters himself or herself.
There is one Dharma, without differentiation.
Distinctions arise from the clinging needs of the ignorant.
To seek Mind with the discriminating mind
is the greatest of mistakes.

Rest and unrest derive from illusion;
with enlightenment, attachment to liking and disliking ceases.
All dualities come from ignorant inference.
They are like dreams, phantoms, hallucinations—
it is foolish to try to grasp them.
Gain and loss, right and wrong; finally abandon all such thoughts at once.

If the eye never sleeps,
all dreams will naturally cease.

If the mind makes no discriminations,
the ten thousand things

are as they are, of single essence.

To realize the mystery of this One-essence
is to be released from all entanglements.
When all things are seen without differentiation,
the One Self-essence is everywhere revealed.
No comparisons or analogies are possible
in this causeless, relationless state of just this One.

When movement stops, there is no movement—
and when no movement, there is no stopping.
When such dualities cease to exist
Oneness itself cannot exist.
To this ultimate state
no law or description applies.

For the Realized mind at one with the Way
all self-centered striving ceases.
Doubts and irresolutions vanish
and the Truth is confirmed in you.
With a single stroke you are freed from bondage;
nothing clings to you and you hold to nothing.
All is empty, clear, self-illuminating,
with no need to exert the mind.
Here, thinking, feeling, understanding, and imagination
are of no value.
In this world "as it really is"
there is neither self nor other-than-self.

To know this Reality directly
is possible only through practicing non-duality.
When you live this non-separation,
all things manifest the One, and nothing is excluded.
Whoever comes to enlightenment, no matter when or
where,

Realizes personally this fundamental Source.

This Dharma-truth has nothing to do with big or small,
with time and space.
Here a single thought is as ten thousand years.
Not here, not there—
but everywhere always right before your eyes.
Infinitely large and infinitely small: no difference,
for definitions are irrelevant
and no boundaries can be discerned.
So likewise with "existence" and "non-existence."

Don't waste your time in arguments and discussion
attempting to grasp the ungraspable.

Each thing reveals the One,
the One manifests as all things.
To live in this Realization
is not to worry about perfection or non-perfection.
To put your trust in the Heart-Mind is to live without separation,
and in this non-duality you are one with your Life-Source.

Words! Words!
The Way is beyond language,
for in it there is no yesterday,
no tomorrow
no today.

Reprinted by permission of the translator, Richard B. Clarke, director and resident teacher at the Living Dharma Center (P.O. Box 304, Amherst, MA 01004)

III: No Way Out

You Are This

Everything points to nothing and is made of that same no thing. This message is not about mental clarity or any sort of "knowing." There is no assertion of path or practice, nor any promise of attainment or some arrival someday at a special state of peace, stillness, or silence. The message is, there is only what is, happening, and this is happening to no one. There is nowhere to go and nothing to become. All there is, is … everything, Simply Being. There is NO actual "eternal state." That's simply a pointer to Self-Shining Empty Fullness. There is only timeless Being and in that timeless Being, there arises the appearance of separateness and it seems there is an "individual" who then seeks for "Wholeness." But there is ONLY Already Wholeness and so the seeking denies that seeker his or her "goal," because that "goal" is what already IS.

There is NO Way Out of Being. Being IS Everything, and No Thing. This. Is. It. Being IS. Being Life, Being Death, and That is all there is. No one gets That. The appearing manifest multiplicity - you and me and world - are in Reality, One Being, Unicity, and there IS nothing but That....

There is only One. You Are This One.

IV: But First, See This:

"The Tao That Can Be Spoken
Is NOT The Eternal Tao"

- *Lao Tzu*

“Realization is explosive. It takes place spontaneously, or at the slightest hint. The quick is not better than the slow. Slow ripening and rapid flowering alternate. Both are natural and right. Yet, all this is so in the mind only. As I see it, there is really nothing of the kind. In the great mirror of consciousness images arise and disappear and only memory gives them continuity. And memory is material -- destructible, perishable, transient. On such flimsy foundations we build a sense of personal existence -- vague, intermittent, dreamlike. This vague persuasion: 'I-am-so-and-so' obscures the changeless state of pure awareness and makes us believe that we are born to suffer and to die."

– *Sri Nisargadatta Maharaj*

V: There Are No "True Words"

Any words written or spoken here (or anywhere else!) will be misleading ... and 100% OFF the mark. Do not believe anything: Root out the "believer" ... that which is false.

"People come here with some profound concept of spirituality. They think they have spiritual knowledge and they want me to give them a clean certificate. This I don't do. I blast their concepts... All knowledge is ignorance".

-Sri Nisargadatta Maharaj

Part One: Pointing To THIS...

What Is Reality?

The appearing manifest multiplicity - you and me and world - are in Reality, One Being, Unicity, and there IS nothing but That.... There is only One. This One is an Empty Aware Presence that never ends and never begins. You ARE this Awareness, Presence ... IN and AS which the Universe and all possibilities arise. All that IS appears and disappears in That. All there is is This One. That is the Indescribable Invincible Reality. You are That.

1. Bad News, Good news

Here is a question for YOU: If you are seeking .... What are you seeking for? What is it that you don't have right now that you want to attain? Awakening? Enlightenment? Self-Realization? Liberation? What ARE these things? Are they "things" at all?

Perhaps the habit is to identify your self as the thought "I" - as in I Am. Notice right now if the Presence behind the I thought has been overlooked. Break into the habit, being aware of That Presence as your True Identity. This takes no time nor practice. It's just a natural seeing ... right here, right now. And that's the end of seeking; the Natural, Eternal Stateless Being has been found to be never missing.

Here's another, harder question for you: What IS enlightenment? What IS awakening? Liberation? Realization? Do you know what these words mean? What the concepts, these words-sounds, are pointing to? Are the concepts describing some actual attainable object? Some "thing" that "you" can "attain?"

Honestly now? Do you REALLY know? Or do you only think you know? Is it really clear or are you only believing a story told by some so-called "awakened, enlightened, liberated or self-realized 'person'!?" Or is it some hearsay, something you read in some "spiritual book" by some "sage", or some "holy scripture" (which are just records of dead words from dead people recorded as the interpretation of OTHER dead people?)

How foolish is THAT!?

Look: I am not attacking YOU. These words are to poke with a sharp pointer at the balloon of concepts (filled often with hot air!) … let's poke a bit at the "culture" of "spirituality" … because that set of cultural beliefs (cultural = cult) can keep the sincere seeker on the hamster wheel of endless suffering and offers no authentic, lasting peace.

There simply is NO such "thing" (key word, thing) as awakening, enlightenment, liberation, or self-realization. These are concepts, ideas, stories; that is all. And a concept will never satisfy your longing for your true nature. The menu ain't the meal!

That's bad news if you're a seeker.

"What!!??" I hear you blurt out. "I am suffering here. Are you telling me that my suffering must be endured because there is no enlightenment and liberation from this endless seeking and suffering?"

No. The notion that suffering must be endured is truly crap.

Now for the good news. The really cool good news is that what you actually ARE is are already awake, already liberated, already self-realized, already enlightenment itself.

There is peace, joy, freedom, wholeness. But that is not a personal state of affairs. What we call "the person" is just a false belief in a separate individual called "myself", or "I", or "me". Let's have a look beyond words: Are you aware that you are present and seeing these words? And the spaces between the words? Aren't you clearly presently aware that you exist? You are? That awareness is itself endless, beginningless, peaceful, silent and open, like the sky.

That Awareness Itself is the natural, eternal state of total freedom … simply, naked being-awareness.

Notice that. That is what is being pointed to with all the fancy words. Drop the words and see that YOU - this naked awareness – IS. THIS is the beginningless and endless True Peace that the seeker yearns for, shining before the mind's stories of "me" and "liberation" and "someday."

This Awareness is always here right now wherever you go. It may have been overlooked as the mind focused on attaining something that was missing, something to solve a problem for a person. But the actual fact is, YOU are Awareness ... and That is never missing. That is a space-like knowing that the mind translates into the words "I AM."

This Awareness is the peace that surpasses understanding; the natural state of serene open seeingness itself, devoid of identification as this or that thing. This Awareness IS Awake, liberated, realized. This Awakeness IS enlightenment itself. It ain't personal. It just IS. It is NOT an attainment. It very simply already always IS. Full Stop.

You are this. There is nothing more to seek. In fact any seeking can only seemingly obscure that, yet ultimately it is impossible to hide from what you are, since you ARE the awareness that sees these words appearing before the eyes.

Awareness IS. Prior to, during, and after everything appearing, all stories, experiences, knowing, not knowing, etc … that Awareness sees all that is happening. Everything happens in awareness and You Are That. Search Over.

You are always aware, always aware of something, whatever is appearing before your eyes and ears; whether that appearance is painful or pleasurable, happy or sad. Hearing, seeing, knowing … all these arise in awareness. Awareness sees, hears. It's the essence of everything and never missing ever.

That is what you are. So you ARE the liberation, realization, awakeness; you ARE freedom itself. Just see right now that the label, the word, is not the actuality. Freedom is NOT a word. NOT a concept. NOT an experience. Freedom IS and you are that.

You (in Truth) are SILENCE ... Awareness Itself. Already free and peaceful. So if that is what you were seeking you can stop now, because you already have it. See this right now for yourself. If you believe that you are anything other than awareness itself, who believes that? Challenge the assumption that you are a thing apart from that ever-present naked awareness.

You are NOT a concept, NOT a belief or a believer, NOT a thing apart from Awareness. You are what you seek. See it now. You are already the enlightenment, the peace, that you have been looking for. That is all there is to "awakening" or "liberation" Seeing that what you are is naked awareness and what you are not is a thing apart from That.

Awareness is always present. It's not present yesterday or tomorrow, or even today. It's always only here now. YOU, as timeless, spaceless awareness that's always seeing, hearing, tasting, touching, smelling, is what YOU are.

All concepts and experiences that come and go in Awareness are totally irrelevant. Nothing that comes and goes can ever touch the Perfect Peace that YOU are...

Just notice, "I am present and aware, right here right now." That's all there is to it. Game Over:

So: Welcome back to the Home you never left.

"Subject-object thinking seems to cover the natural state (awareness). But without awareness, thinking could not take place. Because thinking appears in awareness (like a cloud appears in the sky), realize that thinking in essence is awareness. Understanding this, thinking cannot obscure awareness."

'Sailor' Bob Adamson

2. This Dawns Naturally, For No-One

The seeing of Aliveness Being what IS with no "person being alive" happens totally without any cause ... no-one can make this happen nor can that "no person" attain this ... no amount of meditation, seminar-ing, satsang-ing, self-inquiring, therapize-ing or any other do-ing will EVER "bring about" the dropping of the false into the Timeless Abyss. Recognition of the actuality of Stateless being simply HAPPENS ... to NO one.

No One makes It Happen

This is like any other "dawning" ... for example, there was a happening here, laundry was being done and the washing was forgotten.

There was no sense of anything that needed to happen, and so two hours passed, then "it dawned" that, "Oh, I forgot to take the wash out of the machine and put it in the dryer."

It's that simple! When this dawning happens, it happens to no-one from no-where and cannot be caused. The same is so for "spiritual enlightenment" ... as what dawns on the seeker is (a) that no seeker actually exists at all, and (b) there is NO such thing as enlightenment and that itself is "enlightenment."

So while along the "way" so to say ... there can be a pointing out of the false nature of any individual believed in as a separate entity.

That said: There may well come about a looking into that false notion and seeing it AS false, seemingly through meditation or inquiry or any one of ten thousand other possibilities.

NONE of that has much to do with The Dawn of Seeing with Naked Awareness that there is NO person, and that ends suffering once and for good.

You can NOT make it happen.

That's Bad News.

But you can NOT avoid this dawning.

That's GOOD news.

3. The Bottom Line

Cutting Through The Story of "me"

1. YOU are Awareness, simply being. No one can say they do not exist. That existence, the sense of "I" as in "I Am," is undeniable and inescapable. Try to NOT BE. Cannot be done. So the simple pointer is, what you are is That Presence or Awareness that YOU ARE. Being. Just That! This True You ... BE-ING... is POINTED TO in language with concepts like Impersonal Consciousness; Awareness, Being ... YOU are just THAT, prior to the mind's translation into the thought I Am and I am this or that.

2. You are NOT an "individual." There are NO "individuals" anywhere except in unreal stories. The idea of a separate person is a fiction, a mind-construction, a house of cards, as the story tries to say "I'm ME!" (Unsuccessfully)! This idea of a "me" is ... on investigation ... seen to be a false claim by the thinking machinery to it's own separate existence. This ever-changing idea of a person is simply unreal. WHO says "I'm Me?" The mind.

To be blunt, it's bullshit. The whole fabricated story of me is pure bullshit: all stories of “individuals” is actually a fiction. As Shakespeare said, it’s a tale told by an idiot, filled with sound and fury, signifying … NOTHING.

Look right now! Seeing with naked Awareness, where is any person … unless you (as a mind-identity) think about it? Thoughts come and go. What you ARE NEVER comes and goes anywhere. It is (You Are) fully Here Now and Eternally Free and Clear, Eternally Presence, Shining before the mind.

YOU are not a thought, not a concept, not a feeling, not a time bound entity. You are Awakeness, Aliveness, Presence-Awareness. Just THAT and NOTHING else. The story of "me" ... ANY "me" ... is irrelevant. Let's cut through that crap right now! Okay?

Let's bring this back to the basics: What in YOU never changes? Being-Awareness, just That. That is your True Nature. Where is a separate entity when you are in deep dreamless sleep? Or under anesthesia? There is none. Obviously! But some Presence beats the heart, breathes air in and out, flows the blood, grows new cells and disintegrates other cells, grows hair and fingernails, ages the body etc etc! Who or what is "doing" all that? Not an "individual."

Look and see that you are present and aware right now. That is the "Eternal," The Natural State; there is no other, no attainment, no flashy enlightened state, no carrot on a stick. There is NO someday when "you" will "get enlightened." It's what you are right now. There is no other than NOW. Wherever you are, there you are ... right here. That's IT. Big Casino. You already got it in total and there's nothing more to this Nonduality stuff than that simple seeing, that you ARE. Awareness, Simply That. Period. Full Stop.

In our meetings, there's just friends, sharing what works to end any suffering and recognize that you are already free and clear. Really. There's nothing to get and no one to get it. Drop the belief in "individuality" and there you are, Present and Alive, the Light of loving being, just that, nothing else.

“Doctrines, processes and progressive paths which seek enlightenment only exacerbate the problem they address by reinforcing the idea that the apparent self can find something it presumes it has lost. It is that very effort, that investment in self-identity, that continuously recreates the illusion of separation from oneness. This is the veil which we believe exists. It is the dream of individuality.”

\- *Tony Parsons*

4. What Is This "Ego?" Where Is "It?"

Many teachings seem to indicate that "the ego" is the problem. But what IS this so-called "ego?"

Depends on how deep you want to go... at a superficial level, "ego" is nothing but a three-letter word. Fraught with meaning, certainly, thanks to Freud, among others. Look up "ego" and you find page after page of explanation.

But the simple dictionary definition I like best is just this: "The self, especially as distinct from the world and other selves."

That says a mouthful. "… distinct from other selves …" in other words, separated from everyone (and everything) but itself.

But where does this "separation" occur? ONLY in language. And what is language? Letters. Words. Concepts. Ideas. And what are all those things? Things! Objects. But what are these objects made of? Are they actually REAL? Or is there just a deep-down SEEMINGLY well-hidden moving Energy, a substance that we can call Source or Intelligence or Being (more concepts! It's hopeless, but …) or GOD? There's an "ultimate concept" for you.

So what is actually REAL in all this play of words and meanings? Perhaps this idea of "my ego" is nothing more substantive than an idea, a movement of consciousness, or intelligence-energy, an infinite creative intelligence, bubbling up and appearing out of nowhere? And is there any actuality to this? Any real solidity? Or is this "my ego" simply an assumed identity, an unprovable belief? WHO is this me that has an ego? Where is there any such thing, apart from language? Drop language, look for the ego-me without a word or sound and what do you find?

Nothing.

What if “the ego” never existed? And what if “it’s power” is nothing more than a false assumption? Investigation may reveal the phantom to be a phantom. Have a go. Look into this.

As you look at this idea of a separate "ego-me self," you might ponder, WHO or WHAT is ‘looking into this?”

What are you? Language? Or something (actually no thing) that TRANSCENDS language?

Who is asking? Find out.

5. I Have Destroyed Your Ego!

Once upon a time there was a Great Master who had a few students who lived in an ashram with him. One day, a student who had been "In search of The Self" and seeking final enlightenment and liberation came to the Master and bowed, and said, "Master, my ego is driving me crazy with desires and suffering. Please help me destroy this horrid ego!"

The Master (who knew there was no Master, no Disciple, No Teaching, no Path, and no Goal,) smiled and said, "Go and sit in your room and hunt very carefully and thoroughly for your ego. As soon as you find it, bring it here and I will happily destroy it for you."

Delighted that at last, "the goal is near," the student retired to his quarters and began the process of seeking the ego.

Some time passed, and one evening the student again approached the Master, a look of deep disappointment and despair on his face, tears in his eyes, and said, "Oh Master, I have searched and searched and I cannot fulfill your command, I have failed you, my Master. I cannot find the ego anywhere!"

The Master smiled, gazed into the students eyes and said loudly, "You SEE? I have destroyed your ego!"

Stunned, the student fell back on his heels, then it dawned on him. He shouted, "There never WAS any 'ego'. It does not exist! How could I have believed in a ghost?!" And with that he burst out laughing, and laughed and laughed and laughed. The Master simply smiled and said, "So It Is. Welcome Home, dear boy."

"All is resolved in the Unborn. Never trade the Unborn for false beliefs and empty meaningless thoughts!"

6. YOU

In one of my Newsletters, this appeared:

YOU ... Ever-Present, Naked Empty Awareness ... are akin to the great empty sky in which all that arises -- storms or sunlight, clouds or rain, light or darkness -- is effortlessly allowed, unresisted, unmodified, simply lovingly accepted -- as it is and as it is not. The sky Itself remains clear and lucid, untouched by all that appears within it. So it is with your True Nature of Nondual Clear Presence-Awareness. All appearances of thoughts, feelings, identifications, attachments, aversions, opinions, forms, names -- everything that appears to "manifest" -- simply arise, persist only for a while in apparent "time" (itself an appearance!) ... and then disappear back into That ... the endless Space of Your Own Awareness, just as the clouds and rain, sunshine and darkness appear and disappear in the clear Space of the sky.

An e-mail arrives ...

Charlie, this writing is really excellent. It really points directly at that clear presence which you are, which I am.

Nice job. But of course, it only flowed from that empty space of knowing that is the only reality. Charlie is but an interesting instrument of this expression! Love, Randall Friend

(Visit Randall at "You Are Dreaming" website is on the internet at ... http://avastu0.blogspot.com/.

7. Freedom ....

..... is another word for no one left to choose

If I ask you, "do you exist," you will automatically answer, "yes."

How do you know you exist? Is that a silly question? Or is the question a signpost to a deeper cognition of what you are?

What is aware of the undeniable fact that you do exist? That which is aware of these squiggles on a white background: What is it? Does that notice the space between the squiggles? Or was that obvious space overlooked?

There is presence, awareness. Right? Can you see that without being, awareness, or presence, nothing can be known? Even what you may think is you? Then can you see that presence-awareness comes before all that is present?

What never changes? What is never missing? What has to be there (here) before you know you exist?

Are you a thought? Can your Eternal True Nature ever be something as changeable and amorphous as a thought or a feeling? Look into this and end the search for happiness, peace, love, or whatever you might be seeking that you believe you do not have, Right Now. But right NOW. Then you may discover that there is no "personal entity" to have any "nature" apart from all that is ... "true" or otherwise.

"Who Am I Anyway? Am I my Resume?" This song title from "A Chorus Line" points to a powerful possibility: The idea that perhaps we have mistakenly identified ourselves as our story of me."

What can arise is a questioning of these assumptions, usually prompted by suffering (but not always. Anything is possible.)

But the possibility for absolute freedom from suffering in YOUR life puts in an appearance when there is “the happening of what we might call Grace” ... and when there arises an inquiry, a sincere and earnest questioning, using the simple thought "Who Am I," that investigation can have an amazing power to dismantle the ego-mind that believes it is in charge of it's life, and suffers because all too often things do NOT go "its" way!

All suffering is a call for investigation: Who is suffering? WHO wants 'what is' to be different, better, changed, corrected? Who Am I that wants what is to not be as it is, who believes that IT is "better than god "and believes ... KNOWS! .. that what is should not be?

Paradoxically, no-one can do it owing to the simple fact that there IS no controlling entity. And it CAN happen. So “I” wish this for “you.”

8. "Awakening?" No One Awakens!

Q: I'm wondering if you would share your "awakening" experience with me and also what you experience now? I guess I'm asking for a before and after picture in a way.

Sure. I was sitting in meditation. Then there was no one sitting, no meditation, absolutely no thing whatsoever, and no one to know that there was no thing whatsoever. Yet the Isness of Naked Light was WHAT IS ... NOT Awareness, NOT EVEN NOTHING.

When awareness returned -- Being "aware of itself" -- this was seen (reported on so to say) as absolute freedom, absolute bliss, absolute love. After the "happening," the "understanding" of this Actuality shattered the false idea of separateness, broke into the ignorant knowing-feeling belief that an "entity called charlie" was, as previously thought to be the case, "the self" or "me." It was a shattering happening! When "I" came back "I" (the mind) blurted out (in the head), "WHAT was THAT!?"

This seeing can only be described in "negative" terms: Not this, not that, not anything. In the most profound and unimaginable way IT WAS SEEN BY NO ONE THAT NOTHING IS HAPPENING, NOTHING HAS ACTUALLY EVER HAPPENED.

Really, This is Indescribable. Unimaginable! Words are 100% OFF and totally useless for any "articulation" of This which IS and yet is Unknowable. This is Before Beyond and Permeating all that is. Nothing, Being Everything, is as close as words can get and still they are 100% false. Sorry about that!

9. Snowflakes & People

No two snowflakes are exactly alike, every single one is unique, yet all of them are made of the same essence ... water. Similarly, no two bodymind organisms are exactly alike; even "identical" twins are in subtle ways uniquely from each other, yet ALL are made of the same essence ... no thing bubbling up into energy-aliveness.

That which is the essence of all that is, is utterly Indescribable and unimaginable. The happening of This is Being ... being Nothing Being Everything. This is Absolute and unknowable ... "You" ... and All that is ... ARE This. Aliveness, Being, and, apparently, happening as everything that appears.

Period. Full Stop.

10. The Great Perfection ...

... is Pure, Non-conceptual, Self-Shining, Ever-Fresh, Naked Presence-Awareness... just That and nothing else.

If you are seeking truth, God, Completion, Wholeness, Love, Peace, Fulfillment ... here is a question for you:

What makes you believe in your own separate existence? What force or power is creating this false cage of conceptual limitation to the Eternally Peaceful True-Nature of all that is?

Find out! Let's uncover that energy that moves the stars and makes the Sun burn in perfect brilliance and superb beginningless endless Silence.

WHAT makes you think you are NOT the Whole Eternal Totality? What has you accept any idea of lack or limitation to your own Incandescent Loving Spacious Being?

What are you? Who are you in Reality? Find out ... and Meet Your True Self in Absolute Freedom ... Right Now.

YOU ... Ever-Present, Naked Empty Awareness ... filling itself with its own aliveness ... are akin to the great empty sky in which all that arises -- storms or sunlight, clouds or rain, light or darkness ... is effortlessly allowed, unresisted, unmodified, simply lovingly accepted ... as it is and as it is not. The sky itself remains clear and lucid, both untouched by, and accepting naturally, everything that appears within it.

So it is with your True Nature of Nondual Clear Presence-Awareness. All appearances of thoughts, feelings, identifications, attachments, aversions, opinions, forms, names ... everything that appears to "manifest" ... simply arise, persist only for a while in apparent "time" (itself an appearance!) ... and then disappear back into That.

THAT is the endless Space of Your Own Awareness, lovingly accepting as its own Self-Expression ALL that appears everywhere, just as the clouds and rain, sunshine and darkness are accepted as they appear and disappear in the clear Space of the sky.

Nothing lasts forever. ONLY Nothing lasts forever. You are That. No Thing. Free and clear, standing outside Creation and embracing all that is.

Be what you are! You are not an object, and not a subject.

You are. Naked Vibrantly Alive Awareness. Nothing Else.

11. A Key to The Kingdom

Investigate. Does this "I" or sense of "me" that has been accepted as what you are actually have ANY control over what thoughts arise, what feelings or emotional experiences come up, what happens in its world?

The key to seeing that this "I" is a powerless concept is, try to control your thoughts and never have an unhappy thought or emotion for, say, two weeks.

Then let me know how it went and if you still believe that "you" are the "managing director of your life."

And while all that is going on, just notice that the awareness of Being, present as the ever-knowing consciousness of THE NATURAL KNOWING, "I AM," has never gone away.

Awareness is never lost nor found. IT IS. That is what you are ... the aware presence that sees thoughts, feelings, changes, happenings, effort and struggle, trying to control, trying to not control ... all is witnessed by that Awareness that you are.

So you are what you have been seeking.

Consciousness is all there is, and you are That.

Full Stop.

When Nothing Meets Nothing,
Everything Is Seen ...

By No One.

12. The Source of Suffering

Perhaps it is simply an unseen background assumption, deeply hidden from apparent view: I am a separate body and/or mind ... "bodymind" ... an object with limits and vulnerabilities in a world of sometimes friendly often hostile "other bodyminds" ... and myriad other things "separate from me."

Call it "mistaken identity." A belief, so deep as to be hiding under feelings and thoughts ... yet at cause in the matter of suffering like depression, despair, sadness, feelings of unworthiness, insecurities and feelings of vulnerability.

To paraphrase a sincere spiritual text, nothing that can be threatened is actually real. And nothing unreal can actually exist. The direct cognition of this fact reveals the Always Fresh Ever Present Peace that Surpasses (Transcends) Understanding.

A body certainly can be threatened, can be hurt, can die. And it will die. That's a given. The question is, am I, are YOU, the body? Or is that identification merely a deeply held conviction, a belief, a thought, idea, words?

Without thought IS there a body? How would we know? We only know what is assumed or what others have told us. On looking deep in the space of awareness, can you find any such thing as a body or mind, unless "you" are thinking it up?

What never changes? What is always present?

What is That which was the same when you were two or three or ten or twenty years old? Has that ever gone away or changed in any way? Bodies change. They grow, then wither and die. Have you noticed? Finding that which never ever changes to be what you are and seeing that the idea of your identity as a changing dying body is FALSE is what can be called " liberation."

That Unchanging Being is Home ... the home you never ever left! Everything Appears in Timeless Peace. That is Real, That is True, That is what you really are.

Don't refuse to be That.

13. Are You Hearing What's Being Said?

I feel like every question that I've ever had has been answered repeatedly over and over again throughout the books I've read on non-duality (from authors like Ramesh Balsekar, Tony Parsons, Leo Hartong, John Wheeler, Nathan Gill, David Hawkins, etc., etc...)

Powerful company you're keeping. Are you hearing what is being said? Or merely trying to fit it into your self-concept of a believed-in "personal entity?"

But even though I understand it all very well intellectually, that there's no separate entity, no 'thinker' behind thoughts or 'doer' behind actions, and all that exists is THIS Presence-Awareness... there is still the experience here of a separate personal "I", or a "me". So the only thing that seems appropriate is to let life flow spontaneously as it always has and just wait things out... <u>but,</u> of course, even then if there's no such thing as a future 'time', then "waiting for enlightenment to happen" becomes just another concept in the present moment appearing on the Screen of Awareness. ... that's sort of where 'I' am at. Any comments???*

*The mind always has a "BUT"! That makes YOU the But of the Cosmic Joke... because you already ARE That which you seek. Always have been!

The notion that the "I" will disappear is one of what might be called the seeker's myths of self realization. The I is no problem. The sense of being a "me" is no problem.

The only niggling remnant here was the idea that the I thought needed to be somehow annihilated ... but by whom? It's a fiction trying to dispel a ghost.

For “me” - the organism appearing “here” - the final clarity on all this came through simply seeing that the I is only an ephemeral appearance, a thought that comes and goes. There's no issue with that: The issue seems to be in the taking that thought on board as our identity rather than simply knowing once and for all that This Presence, the Awareness that is the formless timeless backdrop, is the only true Reality. YET that clarity of “my” being only Awareness-Presence, when merely an “enlightened belief”, is NOT the ACTUALITY of TRUE BEING, which has NO opposites anywhere. THAT is no-where and every-where ... so to speak (words always fail ... always!)

What NEVER changes? Only That can be the Real. So the IDEA of a separate person can come and go (and will!) so long as the Aliveness of Presence is appearing as the organism ... and the clarity of this seeing is that there's no false notion that anything in this appearance should be different ... including the idea of personhood!

The I thought is kind of like the idea that the earth is flat. Just an idea ... a movement of energy arising as thought. Once it was seen to be only a belief that the earth is flat, and not the reality, that idea was no longer taken on as the reality of the earth.

Similarly, if someone in Bombay said hello to Nisargadatta, he would say hello back. But he knew full well he was npot that thought of “I.”

You see, the organism functions as it always has, only the identification as that I-person is seen ... KNOWN ... to be false and so is no longer believed in.

This knowing is direct, immediate and incontrovertible … yet devoid of a knower and an object known. What’s real is the know-ING.

Here's a question: What can you locate anywhere anywhen that is NOT an object appearing to and within the Awareness that you are? That which never changes is ordinary awareness. This ordinary Awareness - your undeniable inexhaustible ever-present being-knowing-loving-to-be ... IS the emptiness of cognizing presence and fullness of all there is. Everything/Nothing.

So I would suggest that, if you still think you are an individual with volition, have that "you" drop the search for someday, drop the label "intellectual" and leave it at "The Understanding" ... which is the pure aware knowing that yes, "I AM" IS, existence itself. That I AM only POINTS to the Truth ... simply don't mistake the signpost for the actual... you know this.

The search is over when you stop attaching to objects and know thyself as the Subject in which (and as which) the objective "world" appears... observer and obeserved are not two.

Take up your existence-presence-affinity as an identity your actual Self, in and as this Unbounded Awareness Itself, and refuse any objective thingness-identification whatsoever.

The Absolute is called Sat-Chit-Ananda, which I translate as Being-Awareness-Aliveness. YOU ARE Just this and no thing else!

If you have a copy of "I Am That" you might like to re-read chapter 44: "...the world of Absolute Reality, onto which your mind has projected a world of relative reality is independent of yourself, for the very simple reason that it is yourself."

Look where THAT one points, without trying to comprehend it or fit it into the framework of concepts and the false reference point that springs from the pure unsullied 'I Am' Consciousness!

You are quite right in the seeing that all ideas of goals like "enlightenment" or "liberation" are conceptual creations.

The mind seems to have an endless capacity for constructing ideas and relating them to other ideas, all ultimately 'belonging' to a "me" ... yet all are merely appearing like puffs of clouds in the Ordinary Everyday Ever-Fresh Awareness that you actually are, to be a bit redundant!

Please do feel free to write again. Let me know how all this vibrates and resonates in the I Am "over there ..."

14. The Screen Of Awareness Is Like A Hologram

Q: have been mulling something over since our meeting last Sunday. I'm wondering about something. Three times during the meeting, I experienced what you call a "mind-stump."

That is what I refer to as a "Full Stop:" When there is a pause of thought-feeling stories, and the mind is in abeyance, there is Naked Awareness. Just That. That is what you actually always are....

In this pause you don't fall apart. So it is seen that Presence-Awareness, the non-conceptual holographic appearance of beingness, that which is labeled by the mind as "I am," IS the ever-fresh ever-present Reality beyond the mind. (This is seen, but not by the person, because the "person" is naught but a thought, and in this full stop there is no person.)

This Self Shining Presence is like the empty (yet multi-dimensional) screen on which the movie appears. The thing that makes this illusory dream appearance so believable as "our reality" is that the "screen" is actually not flat; it is multi-dimensional. So it's more like the metaphor of the hologram. And Being, the Absolute, is like the Laser light. That light of Being-Awareness-Presence is like the hologram's laser light without which the hologram has no independent reality or actual substance. The hologram can't appear without or apart from the laser light. Like that, Presence Awareness is the Light which IS the actual essence and substance of all that is, and the appearance ("life") is both apart from that (seemingly) and an aspect of that (actually.) These are NOT TWO.

You will never grasp and own this with the mind! Don't try to analyze the pointers; LOOK where they are pointing.

This appearance has NO actual independent existence apart from Presence Awareness. And what you call "I" or "you" is ALSO an appearance and has no finite actual existence apart from that Presence Awareness.... When this is seen, and when the false belief in a separate "me" entity is finally seen as false (like a 'flat earth') then it's game over. From then on there is unshakable peace and natural acceptance of what is, when there is the seeing that what you are IS the silent screen on which life happens. That Awareness Presence Silence is FULL with Loving Being This ... appearing and disappearing in a phantasmagoric display. What a show!

Q: Was this something that you intentionally did with me or was it just a result of our conversation? I've been discussing this with some friends to enlighten them and began to wonder if you knew this was needed for me or what.

There are some false assumptions at play here. First off there is the assumption that there is a separate entity called Charlie who has an agenda or intention. This is NOT the case here. What is said is said with no purpose, intention or goal. All that bubbles out of the mouth here is pointers to That Indescribable Isness. You are like so many looking at the pointer and trying to figure out if there is some purpose, intention, or desired outcome on this appearance's part, and there is not. There is NO person with any agenda here; only "Oneness Expressing to Oneness." Dear Oneness: There is NO "enlightened teacher" trying to "enlighten" anyone. Yours Truly, Oneness.

The second assumption is that there is an entity called by a name who can "get" this. There is NOT.

There are no actual separate individuals, not here, not there, not anywhere. All there is is what's happening, including words and music!

In the conversation pointers are shared. Perhaps insights happen. But these are NOT *actually* connected; there is no actual cause and effect relationship at work anywhere. That idea is only a story (the tale told by an idiot!)

It is Heart To Heart, not "person to person!"

I do know this much........I learned from the mind-stumps and thank you for that.

You are very welcome. But NOW: Let's have a go at UN learning now. Fair enough?

What is at work there is a mind trying to grasp, to learn, to collect more data, to add to its store of (false) knowledge. Try on that all knowledge is actually ignorance. I invite you to join me in Unknowing.

Not Knowing, there is Peace. Not knowing, there is Silence. Not knowing, there is Love. Unconditional, unfettered, unencumbered Love, with no attachment or aversion to ANYTHING.

15. Shift Happens

M.H. Writes, *I have been reading whatever I could get my hands on re non-duality over the past 3 years. My first introduction to non-duality was through reading Tony Parsons and 'Sailor' Bob Adamson. I have also been lucky enough to go to some talks and a residential with Tony.*

You are hanging out with the BIG dogs!

In recent weeks there appears to have been a shift where there seems to be a recognition of the oneness in everything. So if I look at a tree, it is seen as oneness treeing, or a person as oneness personing, pain as oneness paining etc. As you know this is the type of language Tony uses. There does appear to be great relief in this, in that the search is not as intense as it has been for as long as I can remember.

And that is a happening in what you are … non-conceptual, cognizing emptiness. That is beyond experience or story. Experiences, when taken to be the seeker's holy grail, can be confusing: This sure FEELS like liberation. But in this so-called Final Understanding or Liberation there is no separation, and no entity to "know" that Oneness is treeing or personing etc. Those ways of pointing to what IS are ONLY pointers and not to be taken on board as some "reality" or "attainment" of, or for, "one," or (even) "One-ness!"

This whole subject-object illusion can get very subtle and sophisticated but WHO is experiencing or knowing or seeing? There is still a false idea of separateness in this whole wondrous experience and story.

However something still puzzles me.

Puzzles WHOM? Who is this "me" that is puzzled?

When I read Sailor Bob, he talks about, the sense of I am, and the importance of staying with that.

The "I Am" Bob is referring to is NOT the conceptual thought form ... the thought "I Am" is NOT a "personal entity." That's a thought and as Bob notes over and over, the thought is NOT the actual. The thought "I Am" is NOT the Pure empty I Amness of Awareness, any more than the word "coffee" is the actual liquid stuff.

In Reality, Presence-Awareness, there is no triad of "knower, object known, process of knowing." That is a false belief pinned to an idea of a separate "me" entity. This Awareness-Presence is Impersonal Being Itself.

This silent spacious know-ING I Am-Ness IS. It is the very Existence of Aliveness Itself. Non-dual and non conceptual, undeniable and unknowable. Incomprehensible to the split-mind ideation of "me/other-than-me." That ideation arises in This Being that is always so, always only reality, always ever present and always new, fresh, alive and full on at all apparent times. Timeless Spaceless Isness ... the word is NOT the actual, look back from behind where the words point and it is seen ... by no one.

THIS ... Non-conceived I AM ... is the silent know-ing of self-shining Empty Beingness.This emptiness is all there is. "Emptiness is Form. Form is Emptiness." NOT TWO.

When I try to sense that I amness, it is felt as something very vibrant, spacious and alive. However it does feel as if there is an " I" doing it.

Okay. Find this “felt I.” Investigate. What is it? Where is it?

Is it actually real or merely a movement of thought-sense-feeling ENERGY? Aliveness patterns as thought, sentience, sensation, subtle feeling-knowing. What is the fuel that powers all that? When you are asleep at night something beats the heart, breathes the lungs, grows some cells and disintegrates other cells. All this happens without “you.” What power is That which wakes up and knows - and then says - I AM?

It seems to go, I, I Am, I Am Me, I Am a name, a body, a mind, a separate entity ... apart from a world “out there,” I am and the world is, they are two. All that is false. The Real is that Power that fuels everything, including the “ignorance”.

Full Stop.

Uncover THAT through rigorous investigation. Now look: Of course it is essentially 'true' that there is no one to do or not do that. BUT don't take that Transcendent Truth to be something you have attained or that you own. The paradox here is, so long as there is the belief in a separate one who is a 'do-er,' that can, and usually must, be investigated and found to be false. Starting from the fact that Being IS what never changes, and that this unchanging essence IS what is real, and that 'you' are already and always only THAT, then if the belief in a 'me' persists put it into the fire of the question:

WHO or WHAT IS THIS I or ME? Where is it? Is it always present or does it come and go in silence? ASK. Seek the source of this Power and find Your Self … unknowing alive awareness beingness. NOT TWO.

Don’t believe any of this. These words are pointers ONLY. NONE of this is “TRUE.”

The sense of I am-ness comes and goes very quickly and there is a sense that I am trying to grasp it.

So stop doing that! CAN YOU? Try! Then it may be seen that all that happens, happens ... without "your" will or volition. And all that happens appears to happen on the silent screen of self-knowing self-shining space-like Awareness-Presence.

So there is a me trying to allow this sense of I am-ness to come to the surface and live from that.

Is there? Challenge that assumption. "Me" is a concept. What you are has never been a concept.

What NEVER comes and goes, even in deep sleep? Have your stand there (here.) Then drop that as well … if you can. See that all this happens in that very ever-present cinema-screen-like Awareness-Spaciousness that is NEVER turned on or off, even in deep sleep!

It feels contrived and a little unnatural.

To WHOM?

There is more a sense of a oneness and " Not two", in the recognition (if that is what it is) of Tony's description of oneness and beingness.

Again, for WHOM?

I am just wondering if this is something you came up against?

Yes!

I know you speak very highly of both Sailor Bob and Tony and would be very interested to get your take on this? I appreciate your time and all the help you have given me in my search. Thanks.

There is NO difference between "Sailor" Bob, Tony, and YOU in Reality ... NONE. All differences are only a thought-feeling-sensing-perceiving story ... the "tale told by an idiot, filled with sound and fury, signifying ... NOTHING", in Reality.

Drop all these separations and false distinctions. Investigate who believes he or she is apart from a Bob or a Tony? All these corpses are animated by One Essence. Find that Essence, your very Self, and all these false ideas and queries fall off naturally and all that is left is what you already are right now – Presence-Awareness, just That!

There is nothing this bodymind would rather be engaged in than this powerful looking and sharing. (Yes, there are still preferences, but not attachment to them.) Thank YOU for your questions and your openness. I really am profoundly grateful for the clear seeing and the end of suffering that has arisen here and sharing pointers to that with "apparent others" is a great gift in "this boy's life."

Keep that investigation going! Asking WHO is asking these questions? Who is experiencing Oneness, or not? WHO or WHAT is puzzled, confused or doubts its existence as Presence-Awareness? To whom is all this happening? Can I find any "person" in this organism? Apart from thought, where am I? Am I a thought? A feeling? What is it that NEVER changes, and on the blank screen of which all that is appears and disappears "moment by moment" in apparent "time?"

That Thou Art.

The bottom line is this:

The sense of I Am is an appearance, an aspect of The Absolute, appearing as Consciousness. As long as there is a sense of separation, which is merely a (false) belief that this sense of being an individual is what you are, it works (for some, if it happens) to seek the source of that beingness.

The experience of Oneness is part of the dream. Ask yourself this: What is it here, in (so to speak) THIS organism labeled x, which never changes? What never moves yet is the essence of all movement?

Ask You.

In the sage words of Bhagavan Sri Ramana Maharshi:

"The thought 'Who am I?' will destroy all other thoughts, and like the stick used for stirring the burning pyre, it will itself in the end get destroyed. Then, there will arise Self-Realization."

There is a lovely paradox in all this: While there is in Truth no such thing as a separate “I’ and you already ARE what you seek, as long as there is the false BELIEF in an individual “me, myself, and I” then this investigation is clearly called for.

Keep going. Stay in touch, and don’t refuse to BE what you are: Presence-Awareness, Just That.

16. Look For “The 'Me'”

Follow-up from M.H. - *The suggestion you made on your phone call to go look for the "I" triggered a lot of questioning and looking at assumptions I had previously taken for granted. Clearly the "I" was nowhere to be found.*

So far so good! And if that "I" was nowhere to be found, could it have ever existed as ultimate reality? No. It was only a false assumption. A belief the mind held in an entity, despite there being NO evidence of its asserted independent existence.

This coincided with a couple of days where there appeared to be a perception of reality that I had not encountered before. There seemed to be just awareness and everything was part of that, including the person I had assumed myself to be. It was a very peaceful state which lasted a couple of days.

Now a little bit of confusion creeps into this clear seeing: Ordinary Naked Awareness is NOT a special “state” or “experience” that gets made “permanent.” That’s the “holy grail” delusion of the seeker-mind that wants eternal stasis, a mind-state, or a place of all peace no pain. That is NEVER going to happen... what is being pointed to is the Awareness, stillness, silence, devoid of anything, timeless and spaceless yet ever-present as immediate wakefulness AND all that arises within That! THAT is what YOU are in Reality. THAT is NON conceptual. NOT an experience, NOT an object. NOT a perception!! Perception is of a false perceiver. That triad of perceiver/object of perception/perceiving is FALSE. It's imagination only.

In the perceive-ING, ordinary see-ING with Naked Awareness, there is NO subject/object split; that subject/object dichotomy is the false belief in a separate self-center, a locus of attention if you like. The point is that it is all FALSE. All experiences are imaginary and conceptual appearances like dreams in sleep, that come to pass, not to stay.

Naturally when it faded (or I came back), I wanted to maintain that.

That story is ONLY a story and plainly false: IT (Awareness) does not fade. YOU do not come back. You as a separate "me" that "comes back" do not exist! All that is is a bunch of thoughts, based on a belief in two-ness, separateness, me and other-than-me.

I realized however that this was the same old seeking and that anything that was an experience was not it.

Good. Now don't forget that! All that happened is a thought appeared. Then the thought got fixated on as "I." That "I" is ONLY a thought and is NOT what you are, the Ordinary Aware Presence of being in which that thought arrives and leaves like a cloud in the clear sky. As Nisargadatta put it, " What was born must die. Only the unborn is deathless. Find what is it that never sleeps and never wakes, and whose pale reflection is our sense of "I."

In recent days there appears to be just seeing, hearing, feeling etc. It seems it is all happening in what I am.

Right On, That is what is pointed out here.

When struggle, thought or potential conflict situations arise, there seems to be a relaxing back into the seeing, hearing, feeling etc. However I am not doing this. It simply happens.

Your Seeing and Understanding of this is perfect, as evidenced by that sentence. That expression is BANG ON. Full stop right here. Naturally, THAT TOO is merely an appearance in what you are. Awareness remains pristine, clear and untouched by all these movements of mind. All you might be dealing with here is a bit of residual conceptual misunderstanding about what is being pointed to. Naked Awareness IS the seeing, and That is never "off." The idea that there is an "I" "not doing it" is simply another movement of thought-energy arising in the Aware Presence that is the True Reality.

That is NON conceptual, NON experience-able, NOT knowable, not attainable, not separated in any way .... That IS, Simply, Naked Presence, Aware and Self-Knowing. Now you KNOW. Or, more accurately, IT IS KNOWN.

These are labels that point to the unnameable. And, of course, the label is NOT what is being pointed to! To underscore the actuality: Seeing with Naked Awareness is already always happening here and now.

Ordinary Awareness IS. You are That. Just That. Full Stop! You are seeing This clearly now. That is all there is to this! Simplicity itself. Ordinary Wakeful Awareness, Naked Presence – these are pointing to what you ARE.

You are NOT an experience or a concept. This is Not-Knowing Beingness Itself. One-Without-A-Second.

After so much seeking I tend to be a little skeptical about these experiences.

I remember feeling that. But: WHO is skeptical??

However there does appear to be something different about the simple awareness of seeing, hearing, feeling, touching etc. It doesn't appear to be something outside of me that I am seeking, but rather something which includes me and everything else.

Though there is a validity as a pointing to the real in what you are sharing, the idea that there is a "me", and an "outside of me," are merely thoughts, movements of Presence … form and formless are Not Two. Drop all that now; just allow (in a manner of speaking) the natural statelessness of Self Liberation Through Seeing With Naked Awareness to arise naturally as the clouds of thought-forms come and go.

Only THAT … the Awareness that NEVER changes, NEVER comes or goes anywhere, is The Reality of Naked Presence. True Non conceptual Nature, Being, Full On, Just That. Full Stop.

Anyway, we shall see how this unfolds. Thanks again for your help Charlie, and If you have any additional pointers I would certainly be very interested in reading them.

Chew on these a bit and let's stay in touch. Thanks for a good, clear question. Now drop the questions and the questioner and just BE what you are. Naked Aliveness, Throbbing Loving Space-like Presence-Awareness. Just That. Nothing Else.

17. It Is Obvious and Simple

Follow-up from Ireland - M.H. writes, *It seems a new perspective has manifested itself here where there is at times a certainty (not intellectual) of no-body being here and things simply unfolding. I say at times, but this "new perspective" now seems to be more dominant than the old one. There is no efforting or expectancy, things just unfold. This must be what is meant by living in the unknowing. However words and books do not seem to do this justice. It is just too simple and natural for that. In fact there does not appear to be any desire to read any more books on this at present. It just seems to complicate with concepts what appears here now as obvious and simple.*

There is no idea here what is going to happen in the next minute, never mind the next day nor is there any huge concern about it. There appears to be an unfoldment in what " I" am and a realization that this has always been the case. Nothing more to say really. The words just don't do it justice and trip me up. Thanks again for your help and support.

This all sounds spot on. Welcome to Nothing Being Everything ... Home! Love you!

18. This is Just Esoteric Ignorance

M.S. Writes, *I've got something to ponder. What is your take on spirits and orbs? I went to Gettysburg last night and a friend of mine is a ghost tour guide. I saw some real interesting photos of spirits captured on film. My thoughts are that spirits are just another version of oneness expressing in its many ways. But why do some appear and others don't, are they trapped, why do these energies get caught in this repetition? I think I know why but would like to hear your opinion too. Peace and love ... pretending to be M.S.*

Anything can appear ... and does ... in and on what we are - pure naked presence. Anything is possible in a dream.... waking dream sleeping dream, no matter, it's all an appearance to what is real. But all these stories about demons and angels and disembodies spirits are truly a load of esoteric ignorance!

What never changes? That alone is Real. And That cannot be conceived, perceived, or "known" by the thought-feeling-story we call "mind."

All that appears are objects to that Pure One Subject ... and paradoxically ARE that pure One Subject in It's aspect of objects manifesting. All is made of what never changes and only appears to change, like the light forming pictures on a television screen.

In other words it's all One ... and all why questions will only lead to more thought story - the never ending mind-play arising in This One. This is it. There are no "trapped entities." That is a story that is believed to avoid the confrontation that THIS IS IT and there ain't no afterlife!

"It's an illusion that 'you' exist--the entity 'you' is imagined. The imagination that 'you' exist as something or someone separate is the cause of acceptance or rejection of something known. It is illusion telling the story of its own deception. The knower and the known are just concepts seemingly dividing natural non-conceptual knowing. Believing in the thought 'I am' gives seeming reality to the objective world which is constantly changing, yet everything in essence is that changeless natural knowing--nothing else".

– *'Sailor' Bob Adamson*

19. All There Is, Is All There Is

Follow-up from M.S. - *Ok, Nonduality question? Not that I have had any questions or thoughts lately.. but... Do you ever feel like you are just Dead. Night and day seem to blend together, motivation and the get up and go, due to panic, fear etc... is gone. Its nice but at times I feel like I may be walking as the old saying goes on the earth but not of it. Have you experienced this?*

Sounds arising from Empty Sandals ...

Nothing is ever excluded from Oneness.

All there is is, all there is!

Since you, The One, exist, all these dreams and questions and experiences and thoughts and perceptions and emotions or states of mind all must be That.

Not a single thing is excluded in the grand appearance.

Nothing Is Everything, Everything Is Nothing.

NOT Two!

20. El Toro PooPoo

R.S. Writes, *I have been using your pointers for my Yoga Teacher who was a little stuck in her philosophy and struggling. Using your "it's ALL BULLSHIT" pointers, she was relieved there was no-one or someone to give her pointers. I shall take your book ("Perfect Peace") with me next week.*

Perfect! :-)

21. No Way Out

An anonymous "advanced spiritual seeker" writes, *There's running around like crazy --LOUD mental stories of essentials missing, this life not 'right' yet for this character and of course, the character "me" itself being the biggest story, around which the rest depends --who is having a very tough time-looking to circumstances to change for the solution, instead of seeing through the character herself--it just isn't happening!!! Words are read, audios listened to, they're almost becoming just 'sounds', there's such familiarity but...*

The story is all about "but." You are the 'but' of the cosmic joke. You will NEVER get this. There is freedom ... but NOT for "you."

The phantom (me) feels deeply embedded in the core still--thus the pain of doing my life all 'wrong', being without a partner (oh horrors according to the conditioning) or a meaningful career--ALL of which is seen in surrounding characters--so the 'what's wrong with ME'???? story plays and plays and plays like a broken record--and it just plain hurts. I don't want another year of this b.s.

That is what is happening ... Being IS This ... Everything, Happening. And, THERE IS NO WAY OUT. That goes on (seemingly, it's actually a dream-story) until it doesn't. Trying to get out keeps the suffering happening. But there is nothing that "you" can do to "escape..." not because you are powerless ... but because THERE IS NO YOU. The Phantom does not exist yet so long as there is that belief in a separate "me" there will be suffering and that is what is... all there is is what is, Being ... EVERYTHING Who would be able to escape from EVERYTHING? The appearing phantom that suffers and wants out is Being ... No Thing happening as a "thing-apart-from-everything" and even THAT is Being Appearing as That. EVERYTHING IS THAT. There is absolutely NO WAY OUT.

There is watching all of this--but the level of discomfort is indicative of some underlying belief in 'me' and not knowing how to shed this--realizing that "i" can shed the 'i". shit.

I gather you mean "I" can NOT "shed the I." That is absolutely correct. Essentially you are completely screwed. NO escape. REALLY! There is NO WAY OUT! The mind bullshits itself into believing it is watching. That's more of the same! That "shedding this" will never happen. Of course "you" don't know how. "This "you" that pretends its the Real is merely a FAKE. How can a phantom dispel itself!? "You" are dreaming and "you" will NEVER wake up. "Letting life happen" may happen but "you" won't do it. Because that little "you" does NOT exist.

The word "I" is only a conceptual pointer to Infinite Being, the Real You. The little you is a ghost-like appearance that is ignorantly and arrogantly taken to be "me-myself-I." So is the "witness!" The pointer regarding "witnessing consciousness" CAN be and often IS a misleading one because there IS NO such "thing" as either "consciousness" or a "watcher" apart from Being-Awareness. THIS "I" appearance IS Aliveness, Being, Being That. ONE IS NOT TWO. THIS is Nothing and Everything but not two. Don't overlook that word that points to WHAT IS: Everything. YOU are NO Thing Being Every Thing. Before Time, God, Watching, Being, Knowing, Not Knowing, or any other dream IS, YOU ARE. Being is all there and not even THAT! Nothing being Everything. Bottom line is, This IS IT. This -- as it is -- is ALL there is. NO WAY OUT.

Yike! Wow. Got it (no-one got nothing!)

Great! Now stay put. Be as you are, Only Being.

22. The False Individual Will Always See "Others"

A viewer of the message that "There is NO "Eternal State" on YouTube shares, *So is physical pain and suffering happening to no one on Earth? Does no one feel chemicals forced into their stomachs or into their eyes? (all kinds of animals in labs) Does no one feel their legs broken, bound together and their bodies strung up in the market to be bought alive? (dog meat market in China) What about all the torture, physical suffering?*

Who sees "others" … "human others" or "animal others?" The moment there is the idea of "me" … an "I" APART from Wholeness … "installed", in a human brain, there arises the false paradigm of two-ness. "I" and "other-than-I" is a belief and creates a false dream-like paradigm of separation. There is NO person and that is a pointer and NOT some "dogma" to take in as yet another false belief. Investigate: Where IS this "I" apart from "other" … animal OR human? Looking into this from nowhere into nothing is a possible happening, but owing to the brute fact that on investigation there is no person and no-one to be separated from all-that-is, you cannot "do" this ultimately, yet it CAN "happen." This was the experience here and in that direct wordless timeless seeing there is the happening of the end of all suffering bang! Right now!

So long as there is a false context, an assumption of a "me" as a person, these questions go on endlessly and never produce a sense of completion or satisfaction. "I can't get no satisfaction" was a favorite rock song … that one is right on … this "you" can never "get satisfaction" because it simply does NOT exist!

As the poet Wei Wu Wei put it so elegantly, from out of nowhere, "Why are you unhappy? Because 99.9 per cent of everything you think, and of everything you do, is for yourself - and there isn't one."

And for those who mount arguments against the intellectual expression (known in the East as "Jnana" - or "Self-Knowledge), consider this, also from Wei Wu Wei: "Even the intellectual understanding of the inexistence of our 'selves' is a rare and bitter attainment which few even attempt. And that is only the elimination round which qualifies us for access to Reality... Intellectual understanding should be not indispensable to a 'simple' mind, but, with our conditioning, it would seem to be an almost inevitable preliminary."

And so it seems to happen this way in many cases. So don't throw out the baby with the bath water! There IS "No Way Out" of Being; Wholeness IS and is absolutely inescapable AND Unimaginable! Paradoxically, You are Being-Wholeness and THAT is Full-on Aliveness, One-Not-Two … and "you" can never "know" this … and so, THIS is The Gift of Absolute Freedom. But not for "you."

There IS Freedom … but for no "person," no "mind," no "I."

Full Stop!

“The Supreme Subject is unattainable,

unimaginable,

undeniable,

ever present, and

manifest as the thought 'I Am'.”

John Greven

23. ALL Words Are FALSE

D.L. Writes, *I enjoy your videos ... Karl Renz says that humans are only ideas, and people don't write books- reality does. when this is seen, there has to be a smile. Thank you for sharing, but then you have no choice!*

You're welcome.

Question: why do you experience any emotion when you get response from a viewer? you said a lady made you feel a certain way based upon her comments. she has no choice in the manner of her response - she is "apparently" acting in the only way she can - if she could respond another way she would. all life has to act in its own best interest at every moment any response you get is perfect. anything else is an argument with reality and that's the source of all suffering... conceptual thought got man out of the trees and now the tool known as the mind continues to run the show.

Everything arises in presence-awareness. Nothing and no one is taken seriously or personally; that sharing is kind of like a "weather report." The pointless point is that that particular apparent "seeker" got some insight from that video; read correspondence with "D.R." (starting herein on page 132.) Now, not to be an Advaita-jerk, but really, WHO says all this? To merely "believe" some concept like "he or she has no choice" is not what is being pointed to. In imagination "we" (the mind-story I thought, a storyteller of amazing proportion) make the pointers into some truth; there is no such thing as a true pointer! But no one was born anywhere, not a him, not a her, not a you, not a me. All is Being As It Is... appearing as this and that.

No worries. ALL words are FALSE!

Very good.

Okay!

"When the self-identification with the body is no more, all space and time are in your mind, which is a mere ripple in consciousness, which is awareness reflected in nature. Awareness and matter are the active and passive aspects of being, which is in both and beyond both".

- *Sri Nisargadatta Maharaj*

24. The Story Is Irrelevant

D. L. Writes again, "There is a curiosity about the experience of this awakening process - how it is perceived by the biological support unit (so-called person). i have read a small collection of them and they are as varied as the organisms themselves. all are of the greatest beauty, for it is beauty (a la Keats) expressing itself through form. If you care to share "yours", it would be most welcome."

In the life of this 'charliething" John Wheeler, Bob Adamson, Tony Parsons, and a few others, kept pointing out the obviousness of Being Itself ... and also pointed out that the "self-centered" idea of the person labeled "me'" is no more substantial than a cloud of smoke appearing as a word-image from a sky-writing airplane.

Investigating this idea of a person reveals its absolute absence, in that absence there is what always is ... the Presence of Awareness, Being, just That... the recognition dawned (dawns only always NOW) that inescapably, there IS Being-Existence, and That is appearing as Everything ... from Nothing.

This is NOT an "experience of an experiencer," rather it is the direct experience-ING of Life ... Aliveness ... or Life Living It-Self ... through all that appears. This Self-Aware Presence is akin to the empty beauty of a perfect mirror in which all experiences arise as reflections, a play of shape and form with no substance in Reality. All there is is Nothing Being Everything. This is seen (so to say) or closer in language this is see-ing ... for no-one by no-one.

Words cannot but divide this into dualism. THIS See-ing Be-ing Love-ING Is ... Only One-Not-Two.

Totality moves an organism to Self-knowledge, seeing the Real and discarding the false, Nothing happens to No One.

AND, all that is merely a story arising presently in Being-Awareness. "You" asking “you” … "who is curious?" “Who are you”? may bear fruitless seeing.

The false only stands in lack of investigation and when looked at head on from indiscoverable indisputable Naked Being-Awareness, the false is seen as the phantom it actually is. That’s it in a nutshell.

The entire gory story is on my website. But it IS truly IRRELEVANT AND IMMATERIAL! :-)

25. Ask Only About Your Own Suffering

Follow-up from D.L. - *Thanks for your response to last weeks email. Questions:*

1. What exactly happened for you to allow the shift in perception? There must be a single moment when you heard a word(s) and the mind gave up. You mentioned earlier it was talking to [John] Wheeler, but at what point in what Wheeler was saying were you able to see that "I am unborn"?

2. Everything that arises does not last and therefore it is agreed to be unreal. and, nothing can threaten the awareness that we are. So, what (and I appreciate the language issue) allowed the human organism to apparently associate with awareness? Why not the rabbit or the dinosaur?

3. Do you see that, as [Tony] Parsons says, its all a game? Just as life apparently evolves, so must the evolution away from thought - Huang Po discusses this - the source of all apparent evil is conceptual thought. If you give this up (interesting in none of his lectures does he discuss how) and see that the senses connect one to nothing, realization can occur.

This is tail chasing. The story of what apparently happened to "another" is absolutely irrelevant.

Are YOU suffering?

That we can address. But there is no interest here in conceptual explanations or stories.

The mind ("I") will ask endless questions ... WHO is asking THIS? Where is this "ask-er?"

DO YOU EXIST?

Who says so? A self concept that reinforces itself in ignorance! IT says, IAMIAIAMIAMIAM. It's conceptual BULLSHIT!

As to Tony's pointers, you will have to ask Tony.

Do you have a question about YOUR suffering? If not, I respectfully disengage.

26. Words Are Instant Duality

D.L. Writes a Follow-up: *Thanks for your previous responses. I understand all words are lies - instant duality. The paradox of explaining the true through the conceived.*

Paradox? No… impossibility! And it's being seen there, by no-one. Great!

Whatever we are has to be prior to object. What I am is impersonal. Not of this world

Yes, in a way… yet there is no "we" (or, "we" are No Thing Being All There Is.)

When there was recognition of no control over body and the mind has the same source, which is not a me, an appreciation of no-doer has existence. It is that knowing that represents the awareness. Everything appears to happen spontaneously. If there is no doer, then there is no causation. No sequence.

Well said.

Anytime a sense of separation develops it should be accepted by no one as wholly appropriate because it appeared.

Drop the "should." IT IS. What IS is Being - Being Nothing and Everything!

Thanks for your videos. Objects can't express anything, reality does. And all that is an illusion.

Happy Now!

Follow-up #1: *Your message is right on. Thanks.*

De Nada! It's happiness here to note that this is all striking home "over there." Welcome Home!

Follow-up #2: *Thank you Charlie. Because there is no doership, there are no enemies. That is peace. The "me" other minds perceive is not the target. Interesting that all technological and scientific developments regard either making it easier for the body to live or allowing man to escape thought (TV, video games, etc). There have been no advances in dealing with the mind for 500 years. The message you share needs to be brought into schools. If children could get a glimpse of this, the world could change in two generations.*

Or not. Who could know?

Meanwhile, all there is, is all there is!

Part Two:

The Seeming "Process:" From Arrogance to Freedom, "Take One"

From

Something

To

Nothing

To

Everything

27. The "Me" Always Wants "More"

O.J. Writes (no not <u>that</u> OJ!) - *Dear Charlie, thanks so much for the videos you've posted on YouTube. They have given me a lot of clarity. Your way of languaging advaita is very appealing to me, and the understanding that I don't exist arises as I'm being reminded by you. Only the emptiness that form/movement happens over and against [what] really is. And this emptiness has the capacity of knowing.*

Emptiness IS. THAT has NO "properties!" THAT is NOT an "object" and NOT a "subject!" (Not even a Really BIG "Ultimate Subject!") Don't complicate THAT with notions of "capacities" or some "knowing" or any other false notion! Drop all that; it's nothing but spiritual conceptualizing. Totally false.

It is the "I am" before the "thought-I am" as you say, the real isness.

Conceptually correct… NON-conceptually IT IS … as is <u>pointed</u> to with "language." ONLY pointed to as what IS is <u>indescribable</u>, beyond language, <u>beyond</u> both being and not-being.

But still, though I see that this is true and I try to stay there, something also knows that there's more! Right?

No. That is absolutely NOT correct. There is NOT any "something." That's dualism, ignorance, the ignoring of the Real, Unborn Being. Now a little phantom "you" trades the Unborn Eternally Real for a paltry little identity you call "yourself," that "me" or "I" that says "*I try to stay there*" and claims there is a subject-me ("*something*") that "*also knows there is more*." And, when you look for such a thing as "I" or a "knower" apart from IS-ness what is found? Nothing!

Looking, seeing, from Nowhere … Here THIS IS … there is always what IS … and there is NO more than <u>Everything</u>! What "you" are not noticing is what there is still operating there a belief in an "I" that says, "I see" and "I try to stay there" etc.

That "I" is a phantom taking itself very self-importantly to be real and separate from all that is. It's the arrogance of ignorance (not "your personal" arrogance; it's an impersonal delusion personalizing as a thought and feeling sense of a contracted "little me.") All this self-centered striving goes on until this "I" is seen through as a fake and only then (now) is the Real re-cognized as the Eternal Statelessness of Being-Awareness-Aliveness. And no-one can "do" this … because there IS no-one! It happens or not to no-one being everything.

Because Ramana talked about that Nirvikalpa Samadhi, I have this ("demon"?) inside that keeps seeking for that state of not being aware of form/movement, only the absolute, only purity. If you feel like it and have time, please, can you help me by commenting on this?

THIS IS-Ness is NOT a "state!" THIS is beyond ALL "states." Being-Awareness IS and That is Timeless, Spaceless, Unknowable, Unknowing IS-NESS.

Now look: WHO "has this demon?" What or who asks "another who" to "help me?" You tell a story of lies and then believe yourself! That's crazy! Look: Terms of art like Nirvikalpa Samadhi and Sahaja Samadhi are descriptions of what actually already IS, NOT "prescriptions" nor "attainments."

Ramana Maharshi was actually dismissive of Nirvikalpa Samadhi as unnecessary to "realization"… Ramana said, "… there is no good in trance [samadhi]." To a questioner who continued to ask about the importance of such "states," Ramana replied, "If you are so anxious for trance any narcotic will bring it about. Drug-habit will be the result and not liberation."

The urge to get "more" IS the ignorance of a mind that considers itself to be real and so chases its own extinction ("nirvana.") But this is patently impossible since there IS NO separate "I" ... it's a phantom ... "mind" is nothing but a cloud-like phantom of a single thought -- "I" -- which is only an energetic formation in movement of infinite Being-Awareness-Aliveness. "I" is merely an appearance, like water in a mirage. Seekers who get an experience of "trance" in activity ... an EXPERIENCE ... become addicted to that experience; it's no different than drug addiction. And the brutal FACT is that NO "experience" is "the final state" or the sought-after "enlightenment."

The brute fact is THERE IS_no such "state" or "thing" as "enlightenment". Key word: "Thing." ALL "states" come and go and ONLY That which NEVER changes, THAT which does NOT come and go, is the Real. And you are already That so all seeking to "become" or "attain" or "disappear into samadhi" (of any "sort") is what keeps the ignorance up front and seems to obscure the fact that You are already That ... Being-Awareness-Aliveness. You cannot "become" what you already ARE.

Existence IS. Is there a separate "little you" apart from the Whole? That is simply ignorance, a false belief, an assumption that is only a speculation of language by a false entity that asserts its reality but cannot supply a shred of evidence for its solid separate existence as a "thing" apart from Everything. Being IS and THAT is appearing as everything. Even the idea of a "thing" apart! Paradoxically!

So that's all that is seen ... by no-one ... and all notions of some samadhi or "special state" disappear as this is seen by no-one -- Naked, Raw Aliveness Itself.

Where is any notion of any state in deep sleep? The sleep state where "you" are NOT is the closest relative state that points to what is Real and Eternally So ... Nothing ... appearing As Everything. Don't trade That for beliefs!

"Who are you? Don't go by formulas.
The answer is not in words.
The nearest you can say in words is:
I am what makes perception possible,
the life beyond the
experiencer and his experience."

- *Sri Nisargadatta Maharaj*

28. Wanting To Be Consumed By Is-ness

Follow-up from O.J. - *Wow! thanks a lot for this beautiful and in depth lesson! That was very nice of you. It really gave me a punch on the jaw. Because although it's seen clearly that everything is one, the illusion of a me still continues, seeking after something.*

That's Nothing Being Everything! No-one "gives lessons." No-one is "nice to do that." It's all a dream; there is NO ONE. Yet, that appearance will go on as long as it does. There is no-one who can do or not do a damn thing about that ... or anything else. You (the cloud-like appearance of a 'you') might as well argue with gravity … or try to kill the moon.

But this almost knocked me out! Thank you very much. It's like a burden is disappearing.. It's like there is this silent ...wow!!! intense silence, the "is-ness" that you emphasize really is a good pointer, a key!!

This Silence Always IS. The arising of "wow" is a kind of Seeing ... a Full Stop. It may happen that there is the arising, the happening, of refusing of all thoughts and abandonment of any belief or investment in "the seeker-me." That's the "Full Stop." But can a false entity, the phantom-like "me," DO or NOT DO THAT? Or anything else? NO. Absolutely NOT.

But it's still obscure. It's not possible to localize it and go into it! It's everywhere right?

YES, THIS is Everything and Nothing, Everywhere and Nowhere. Now: What arises as a "*but*?" And laments, *"It is still obscure?"* It's closer than your breath, the most obvious of all ... Ordinary Being, Being Everything. Never obscured. Only a "you" thought it was. Believe a thought of "I" or "me" or "you" to be real ... and you are lost in delusion. Yet that too IS a happening IN this Naked Being-Awareness which is NEVER ABSENT. See that right here right now!

Thank you for clarifying so many things. But its flavor gives rise to a sense of wanting to be consumed by it!

Okay, as a kind of poetic expression, this is quite right as far as it goes: There IS the Immensity Of Aliveness ... That's what IS ... and THAT seems to consume all that is false ... AND what gets consumed "against its will" is the one who wants to be consumed. "You" don't REALLY want to "be consumed." That's a lie ... a strategy that the mind-ego employs to keep up the appearance of separateness and self-centered solidarity.

(I'M SORRY!!!) Can I ask how that happened in Charlie? Is there a technique?

What arises as an "I" that says "sorry?" And these "yes, buts?" Who or what believes "wanting to be consumed by it" is somehow wrong and says "I'm sorry?" WHAT is saying thinking writing looking asking "but"-ing etc etc WHAT?? What brought out a "but?" Who says "Obscure?" Obscure to WHO? "You?"

LOOK: This mental thunderstorm storm called "you" is totally out of control! Is that noticed now? LOOK: That false "you" cannot stop the "but" from arising and that phantom "you" cannot erase itself. That false "you" believes it is real and so it believes "charlie" is real and "something happened "in charlie." Now IT wants to know <u>how</u>. IT wants a technique, a process. LOOK: there is no charlie, no technique, no IT. How can No Thing dispel what does NOT exist!? <u>Nothing will work.</u> Nothing.

Nothing "happened in "charlie." There IS NO "charlie." There IS NO "O.J." There IS NO-ONE and NOT even THAT! So "who" or "what" would "employ a technique?" All sorts of stuff can appear to happen like asking who am I? Or meditating...but that's all part of this dream of being human and separated from all that is. <u>Nothing will work</u>. It is absolutely hopeless. In other words, it is absolutely hopeless.

To say it another way, it is absolutely hopeless.

And, Nothing will work. Any "practice" or any "technique" presupposes a "limited, bound 'person' to practice." HOW could a practice that reinforces the false release the false from itself? And watch if the mind-ego says, "well, okay maybe Nothing WILL work." "Maybe "I" can "use" nothing" ..,. “do” “nothing” … as the "technique”...??

It's hopeless! There is NO WAY OUT.

Nothing happens here. Nothing happens there. Nothing could happen "someday." There is NO “someday.” That is the fantastic dream of space-time and location. THIS alone IS … Timeless Spaceless Is-Ness.

This is it. This IS all there is. There IS NO Time, NO "someday," NO "becoming." ALL there IS, IS THIS. Nothing happening apparently as everything apparently being some things striving for no thing. Nothing Being the fantastic (fantasy!) Dream of Everything.

TILT!

Game Over.

"The very idea of going beyond the dream is illusory. Why go anywhere? Just realize that you are dreaming a dream you call the world, and stop looking for ways out. The dream is not your problem. Your problem is that you like one part of the dream and not another. When you have seen the dream as a dream, you have done all that needs be done."

- *Sri Nisargadatta Maharaj*

29. The Questions Can Be Endless

O.J. Follows up with: *Even though deep spiritual insights happen almost every day in meditation, ultimate peace is not found. I am starting to believe that some how I am creating this whole experience, including the so called matter all around me. Is the world - I mean all of material - just my thoughts? I see this "I am" as a very good pointer, and your video on YouTube called "all questions dissolve in I am" is really everything that needs to be said. But questions such as "how come there are eyes and ears and nose?" "How come there is life and death and what will happen after?" It doesn't seem like there's any free will at all, [but] the law of cause and effect is a LAW! But why all of this then? why does God want to suffer? Why cant "I" disappear into nothingness? Why do I feel I'm being guided? ... if you find the time, drop me a word of wisdom or just punch me in the head with something big and verbal. Love and gratefulness...*

What is it that is asking all the 'why' questions?

Seek the source of that which asks for a story within a story within a story. You are Emptiness. Be what you are ... and stop pretending to be the story and the storyteller, and the star of the never-ending story!

Before God is Emptiness is ...This Emptiness is Wisdom and Its Fullness is Love ... This IS You ... and You Eternally ARE. Be as you are. Empty and storyless, Loving the Fullness of Simply BEING.

30. It's Just a Case of "Mistaken Identity"

Follow-up from O.J. - *Thank you! Yesterday everything was clicking, clear. It was so alive, and there's so much gratitude, so much happiness and love, aliveness as you say.*

That is ALWAYS the caseless case. Note that in the appearance of things "you" "come back" (so to say) and relegate this clearness to "yesterday." But where or when is this "yesterday?" ALL there IS is NOW.

These two e-mails from you have brought so much understanding with them, and caused a lot of revelation as to what we are. Nothing. Isness has been the theme of these last days. It's amazing that nothing is!

Equally amazing is that EVERYTHING is.

There's still some unrest in here though, having worries about money and wanting to get out of certain relationships and so on...

That's what is. If there is an idea that it "should be different" then that's the suffering; only a "me" could want what is to be better, different, more or less than it is. What is IS and what is not IS NOT. Full Stop. This IS It. As It is and as It ain't.

...and really wanting to thank some charlie guy it insists exists. So, with danger of spoiling non-duality, thank you so much again. I just want to bow. Wow.

You are just bowing to your SELF ... all there IS is YOU .... and YOU called Not-You. And, Non-duality includes it ALL! That cannot be "spoiled."

Although the I is back today suffering a bit, and the big aliveness of yesterdays blissful high moment [seems to fade] more and more is being downloaded so to speak.

More and more being downloaded? What does that mean? Makes no sense...

Is this how it always goes?

For whom? Where is the "I" that claims it is "back suffering?" Can you find such a one apart from Awareness It-Self? No. Whenever there is wanting of what has passed or is not here yet, or here right now, there is going to be suffering!

When the "I" that wants what isn't is seen to be only a power-less thought-construct, suffering goes, and all there is, is what always already is ... True Peace, Absolute Freedom, Unbound-ed Being Aliveness. If you experience a sense that what is ought to be different there will be suffering; release happens when it is seen that even THAT is part of everything ... what IS ... and then there is a hearty laugh!

Of course there's a wanting to die completely, and it's seen very clearly that that is what has to happen somehow.

To whom? How can that which is merely a wisp of cloud-like thought die? That was never actually born. Nothing is there to die!

There's an urge somewhere to lose contact with the body and be only isness, but the isness is the body of course, though it's a mystery. The bodymind is irritated sometimes with it's so-called girlfriend, but otherwise, things are just great!!!!

All experiences arise in Being ... Presence-Awareness. That is always Here and always Now. Nothing that changes is ultimate-ly real; only Being-Awareness, Being Nothing, Being Every-thing is Real... go deeper into this claim of a "me" that is ask-ing or doing or feeling or wanting to be in control of what hap-pens: What Energy, what Aliveness, drives this? What fuels this? What drives what is felt or thought?

Thank you so much mr. no-one.

Hahaha .... De Nada!

Does the bodymind named charlie always only live totally mo-ment to moment and never plan ahead or worry?

Plans happen. Whether they come to pass is always unknown. A trip was planned to Ireland. The trip was canceled. No one does all that stuff; there is no real sense of being personally "involved" in these happenings ... everything is simply happening in the Presence of Being-Awareness.

There is NO doer in Reality. The doer was a false identity, a mistake made in the mind. So, worry is gone immediately (if it arises at all) as it's seen that there is no person to be concerned about what happens or may happen. All "worries" are about a self-identification called "I am this body" and "I have to make sure I take care of it and keep it safe and secure." That is the suffering of mistakenly identifying as a thing called "me."

You are NOT an object or a thing that can change or be threatened. That bodymind is an instrument THROUGH which Totality Happens. That organism is fundamentally connected to everything that is.

You are Being-Awareness and nothing else ... AND Everything "else." Paradoxically! It's ALL Presence-Awareness; ALL Aliveness. Everything is That. Full Stop.

Consider this, ponder this: As long as you believe this is "your" life you will hang on for dear life to that idea. Because "you" do NOT want to "lose your life." But if there is no "you," who is hanging on to what? It is awfully tiring trying to keep that which you never had! That is a game you are sure to lose. And what makes you keep playing a losing game? Ponder that one.

BE in The Gift Of Unknowing.

31. An Arrogant Mind Says, "I Know"

Follow-up from O.J. - *First, thank you. It's seen now that the I is not a solid object, truly, honestly. You say I am a space, a nothing. This might be so, but so what? nothing really changes, even though the I-thought isn't believed to be my true self, it still comes up, it doesn't die. All of "creation" is one and it looks from where I sit here that all that can be pointed to in the world, is that emptiness masquerading as form, the universe is one consciousness in a sense. But since there's no "I" to do anything - how does everything happen? Is this body just reacting to the rest and the pure emptiness is witnessing? No will anywhere? How come this miracle happens?*

1. Don't believe what I say!! Looking for yourself is what this is about, NOT believing any pointer or any so-called "other."

2. NOTHING happens. All this is about is seeing the false as false and the real as real. Nothing will happen! That's the spiritual bullshit ... waiting for some big enlightenment thing to happen. You wrote, *It's seen now that the I is not a solid object, truly, honestly.* STOP HERE!

3. You still want to know how and why! Asked and answered already. Re-read the previous e-mails.

....and don't think i don't know what you're going to say: "Who's asking the questions? Find the source of this "I". There's nothing there." Yes I get it. But nothing really changes, it won't disappear forever.

The mind is way too arrogant, claiming "I KNOW" what YOU are going to say! Just notice that ... here is what actually is here to say:

The "I" as a thought of sense of being a person need not disappear and most likely will NOT until the physical body dies! All that is being pointed to is a false IDENTIFICATION with the "I" thought.

Seeing the false AS false is what this is all about. Then suffering abates and is finally gone forever as there is no sense that life is happening "to me."

There is Life Itself and you are that, including ALL thoughts. Waiting for the "I" to "disappear" will have that "I" around still "believed in" and looking for its own absence (!) and that can bring suffering. One who waits waits forever. See right now that YOU ARE and THAT is KNOWN beyond doubt.

Everything else is a story and just let the story be without attaching yourself as a person telling a story ... being a story and a storyteller. Let it BE. No resistance no problems! As to saying "I got it," that's just another thought story. Drop it and BE.

Ponder: "In this spiritual hierarchy, from the grossest to the subtlest, you are the subtlest. How can this be realized? The very base is that you don¢t know you are, and suddenly the feeling of 'I amness' appears. The moment it appears you see space, mental space; that subtle sky-like space, stabilize there. You are that. When you are able to stabilize in that space, you are space only. When this space-like identity 'I am' disappears, the space will also disappear, there is no space. When that space-like 'I am' goes into oblivion, that is the eternal state, 'nirguna', no form, no beingness. Actually, what did happen there? This message 'I am' was no message. Dealing with this aspect, I cannot talk much because there is no scope to put it in words."

"The knowledge 'I am' is the greatest God, the Guru, be one with that, be intimate with it. That itself will bless you with all the knowledge relevant for you in the proliferation of that knowledge, it will lead you to the state which is eternal."

- Sri Nisargadatta Maharaj

32. Welcome To The Home You Never Left

A last message from O.J. - *Thank you. Finally, now there is knowing. That was exactly what was needed, at the right moment. These words hit a spot, these words something recognizes as truth. trust happened. you must have understood this body-mind pretty well from these e-mails! Infinite gratitude for your generosity my dear mysterious Internet friend. You have helped a lot in realizing that no mind means no mind and somehow this current of I-amness is seen now. I owe you one man! And thanks for the hit in the head last time too! No questions left! Peace and Love, O.J.*

Excellent news! Welcome to the Home You never Left...

No one owes anyone. There IS no one. And That is That!

All done!

33. The 'Aha' Is Always Here and Now

Hi Charles, a friend suggested visiting your YouTube Videos - good stuff. Question: Was there an aha! that came upon you and under what circumstances?

Yes, when I met John Wheeler. John pointed out the inescapable fact of Being-Existence ... I AM. He asked, do you exist? The aha was that obviously I AM before the *thought* of being "I Am" or a being "a person" ever arises. Then he also pointed out that only a false belief in a self-center, as "me," seems - like clouds *seem* to obscure the sun - to obscure the ever-present Being-Awareness, and that by looking into this belief and finding that it is only a false assumption, the whole paradigm of seeker-seeking-something-someday fades and there is what is Always So ... Being-Awareness-Aliveness... just That ... and it's clear there is NO separation of doer in That.

The subsequent investigation seemed to take some "time" but this seeing was actually really "done" in the instant of immediate and direct apperception. This happens only always NOW; this is a direct immediate seeing by no-one that what IS is No thing ... and That is appearing AS Every thing.

All that happens is (in a way of pointing) a clear seeing of the fact that "story of me" IS ONLY a story and NOT the Real. All the "mind " can be used for is to uncover what is false:"Who Am I?" The Real is Unborn, ever fresh and not only obvious and inescapable right now but also inconceivable and unknowable. That is what IS Prior To Awareness, and allows for the arising of Awareness and the pulsating of Aliveness - Intelligence-Energy, the Unmoved Mover of all that is. In short Nothing Appearing as everything; Pure Wisdom, Pure Love. Seeing this directly as Naked Being, ends the search once and for good.

Thanks.

De Nada! :-)

34. You Are Beyond All "States"

Q: I've just been told about you, this morning. I have read Sailor Bob Adamson, Tony Parson, Ramana, Nisargadatta and very recently Jean Klein.

That's VERY good company you are keeping! You'll hear nothing really different here than what they are pointing you to look at and the essence of the Message is that YOU ARE what you seek. Just noticing <u>that</u> is a fundamental starting point in this.

My stumbling block is on Enlightenment. Since we have to use words to exchange, with their limited conceptual interpretation, I will use the word "State".

There is NO "state of enlightenment." "States" are experiences in awareness that come and go. The classic example is of the "sage" who asked for a bowl of rice to be brought to him. Then while waiting he meditated and entered a "state of samadhi" (so-called transcendental union or oneness) … then he came out a week later, in an empty room, and looked around and shouted, where's my rice? That state passed as all states must. What is it about "you" that NEVER changes? Look at that one.

What we call enlightenment here is the simple seeing that <u>only</u> what never changes … your inescapable Being-Awareness-Aliveness … is Real. ALL that comes and goes is a dream-like appearance arising out of nowhere in the Absolute Being-Prior-To-Awareness … and That is the ONLY unchanging Reality … the so-called Eternal State. This all appears in YOU, as Being-Awareness holds all that is like an infinite unbounded "bowl." (The use of the word "state" here is poetic. It is really more accurate poetically pointed to as "The Stateless State." Words divide the whole, but only apparently!)

You are dreaming that you are awake, dreaming that you are asleep, dreaming that you are dreaming. All three "relative" states of Consciousness are dream states arising, as already said, IN or ON the Absolute Unknowing Being that you truly are.

The "idea of you" appears in THAT … the Timeless Spaceless Unborn Absolute You… words seem to make That an object known by a subject so do recognize that all words only point to That which is ultimately totally BEYOND describing or representation and CANNOT be grasped! In short do NOT believe or accept a word of this or any other pointer as some "truth."

I understand what you and the others are saying.

WHO understands? Where IS this "understander?" This is NOT a matter of mentally comprehending. When a false "you" listens as "an individual" hearing another false "individual" say this stuff, the message is completely missed! All you will read or hear here and from the others you mention is I AM speaking to I AM. The ONE I Am of Being Itself.

But I am looking for that state where the illusion, the dream is "really" seen through. The state that Robert Adams, Bernadette Roberts, Jean Klein, Ramana etc. experienced.

Again: There is NO permanent "state" to be "experienced." What is being pointed to is as stated many times NOT an "experience!" That cannot be stresses too strongly. NOT an experience. YOU are NOT a concept NOR are you an "experience." You are NO THING and until that is fully understood there is no end of seeking states and blissful experiences and all that crap! It is, to be straight about it, a bullshit story, a myth.

See, I have the knowledge that you are talking about

This is the mental comprehension and that is the booby prize. You must go a LOT deeper. This "having knowledge" or "owning the concepts of knowledge" is superficial and cannot dispel suffering. WHO says "I know?" Where is the "me" that asserts, "I have it?" What is it that wants a "state" that this false "I" can own?

Where IS this I, this "self-centered entity" called you or me, with a name, and desires, who wants, and wants, and wants ... always wanting what is not already always here?

... but then this doesn't come with the state of these individuals, of Buddha...In Tibetan Dzogchen, they give the example of the clouds obscuring the sun. The clouds being the obscuration of the mind, the ego.

That is a POINTER. But this obscuration is UNREAL. We make it real then try to dispel it! That is tail chasing!

They give many, numerous methods, techniques, mantras etc...etc. to enable one to reach this state. They called this state "Rigpa".

All that is in my view a corruption of the simplicity of this. The word Dzogchen translates as "The Great Perfection." Then that is defined as "Ever-Fresh, Self-Shining, Non-Conceptual, Presence-Awareness, Just That and nothing Else." THAT is ALL!

Notice that the ego is taken to be a "fact" where it is only an assumption of a belief in something unreal. This so-called "ego" is a fantasy, and that is NOT real to begin with! Then all manner of practices are "prescribed" to annihilate this fantasy of a false ego. But since the practices assume the fact of an ego and thereby only reinforce the illusion, how could they take the ego beyond itself? It's a totally false assumption, a faulty premise, operating unnoticed in the background of all that story of practices leading to perfection "someday!"

Where IS this ego? Can you find one anywhere? (See chapters 4 and 5.) Apart from a simple one-letter thought ... "I" ... which is merely a cloud-like appearance assumed in ignorance to be a thing apart from the whole, there is NO ego, and NO separation, only an IDEA of such. Can an idea, a thought, separate itself from the aliveness, awareness, in which it arises? And what is at work here that is driving the appearing thoughts of "me and the universe?"

Where is a me apart from that infinite Energy that drives totality to appear as manifestation and seeming (ONLY seeming!) separate objects and separate pseudo subjects? Subject/Object … "I/Other" … IS the core delusion.

The ego is then dissolved, what Ramana experienced as the death of the ego.

Actually that's a descriptive kind of "poetry." But it's absolutely NOT "the truth." How can a non-thing that never really existed in the first place die or be dissolved? It might feel like dying when identification is strong due to force of habit. But it is still false! No matter how "real" it "feels."

It seems to appear as fading or dyong in the waking dream as a seeker's sense of separation fades … either gradually or suddenly. But when the premise or assumption driving the question or statement is wrong the answer or conclusion will also be wrong: If there is no such thing as a separate "person" how could that nonentity die?

Does just "abiding in this "knowledge" lead to the "blissful" fully Realized state?

Abide as what you ARE … No Thing. That is already "bliss." Empty Loving Spacelike Being. The personal "you" was never born! That Absolute Being-Awareness-Aliveness IS all there is. All there is IS all there IS ...You in Reality are already fully Realized.

You are Nothing … appearing Nowhere … and Everywhere … as … Everything. There is NO path, NO goal, no knowledge, nothing to get and no-one to get it. Full Stop.

35. Don't Be Lazy To Investigate

H.M. Writes, *Do you know, it's really frustrating to hear you and others speak words of truth; to be reminded of a very dear friend who said much the same 20 odd years ago and still to be sat here holding onto the belief that I am what I am not and to know there is not a damn thing "I" can do about it.*

That's not actually true. What that "you" CAN do is LOOK into this story of "me" with a direct challenge to the assumption that there "Is a Me" and That Thought of I is what I am. That assumption is false as you can easily prove by actually looking into the space with a couple of simple questions. But first, can you NOT be? You ARE and THAT is inescapable. Start from that certitude.

Then if suffering or frustration is there, for whom? Where is the "self center" - the "me" - that keeps reasserting that "I hold onto that belief in a separate entity?" Ask YOU, WHO AM I? Where is this "me?" You look and see in the immediacy that there is only a temporary thought that is not always there and is completely gone in deep sleep wherein the body is lived by Being-Awareness-Aliveness just fine!

Do NOT be lazy to investigate and root out that core false assumption! Read the other correspondence on my site, and stay with I AM ... Being-Aliveness ... and let THAT show you the infinity of Love and the emptiness of the Self. You were never born. Being The Unborn is Freedom and You Are THAT. Do not refuse that and do not pretend to be a little separate thing apart from That.

While it is "ultimately true" that there IS no "you," as long as there is that appearing belief, investigation can (and usually MUST) happen.

36. Oneness Urges "Connection" To ItSelf

Q: Felt the urge to connect, but don't know what to say. Maybe it's just time to have the ego be completely disregarded again. The pointers are going okay I suppose. Like "I" could tell. It seems like a bad idea to try to talk about what's going on because it just reinforces the seeker identity.

That urge comes from Oneness ... the Truth wants only Itself. And as John Wheeler quips, "The Path Is A Truthless Land." ALL paths lead "somewhere" ... the Truth of Being Awareness Aliveness is Right here Right Now and That is THAT. Ha! "*Time to have the ego completely disregarded?"* That is just another story of an uninvestigated storyteller … does that "I" telling the story actually exist? Where is this infamous ego that needs disregarding!? Is there any such thing? Or is there just Space-Like Awareness and a thought taken to be "who or what you are?" That is simply the Case Of Mistaken Identity! NOW quite possibly there will be a seeing from nowhere by no-one that even THAT is (inevitably and always) yet another aspect of what YOU really are, which is … Ta Da… EVERYTHING! That does NOT mean that there is everything and then apart from everything there is an "I." Seeing this is the so-called "final understanding" ... not a mental comprehension … this is direct know-ing without a know-er: Apperception.

A reminder from Sri Nisargadatta Maharaj: "One in a million will listen, understand and abide by the advice of the Guru, that 'you are everything.' He or she accepts with conviction ... [but] in most cases, the beingness assumes that it is a body that has taken shape, so one believes that he or she is born and will die. ... there is no death and no birth; one can never be born and die." The pointer is, BE that "One In A Million!"

Thinking about it and making up stories about it and trying to understand it are all not very helpful. Like the end of that [Bob Adamson] *clip you sent, just ideas chasing ideas.*

Yep. So simply STOP the habit in its tracks: As long as there is ANY vestige of belief in a "you" put that "you" to the task of Self-Discovery through absolute unswerving commitment and uncaused intention! Refuse to buy the con man mind's game of separateness and suffering. Watch the thoughts as they come and go in Presence-Awareness and don't latch on to any thought as being you or meaning something about you... that is all. Break that habit right now!

I do have a question on the pointers. You wouldn't think something so simple could be done incorrectly, but I've discovered there are a few ways to do "who am I". One way, which I think you were saying in the conference call, is after asking "do I exist" you look for the "I" in that place where you see directly that you exist.

What is this asking? Where is the ask-er? What says "I" over and over and over? WHAT is THAT? Where does that arise from and subside back into?

Ask the self-concept, the "I," ... Do I Exist? There is ONLY the QUESTION.

If you look for an answer you are sticking yourself back into ignorance.

Ask "you," Do I Exist?

No Answer. Ask with NO expectation or agenda to "get somewhere." You are already HERE NOW. You ALREADY ARE what the mind seeks.

Do I Exist?

Do I Exist?

Do I Exist?

Do I Exist?

Do I Exist?

STOP!!!

Like just asking "do I exist" sort of throws you back into "that" and obviously there is no "I" there. Another way is looking in the mind and seeing the "I" come up and seeing it is just a thought. Does it matter which way you do it or are both effective? Or am I way off track and need to be pointed back to the pointers?

I -I- I- I- STOP! What "throws" who into what? You are already THAT.

Anyhow, it's been back to basics here. Pondering the fact of my existence, which really is quite amazing. Also, after the mind exploded last week, things have been subtly different.

Once the seeing has happened there may "seem to be a "flip-flopping" into identity and back out of it, but you can never again take it as seriously as you did before the mind collapsed in the First Instant of Timeless Being.

I thought about you on your birthday and I hope you had a good time.

No-one was born. Yet a good "time" was had here by no-one!

I'm going into a meeting now. Don't blow my mind while I'm in there, okay? ;-)

WHAT "mind?" Show "me" a "mind" and "I" "won't blow it!" LOL.

Ponder this… which was written today to another "seeker" … "all you are facing is habits of the brain that is accustomed to thoughts of me myself and I.

"That was gone through in the charlie thing... it came to pass ... the investigation happened and all the story was seen as false, as is the story-teller.

"Break the habit. It takes intention. It takes your commitment.

Self-Knowledge is NOT a trivial matter!"

It takes all you can muster ... paradoxically for when you look there is No “you" but as is said over and over so long as there is that belief in a "person with will and volition" put that "person” to the task of questioning its very existence!

To repeat what Nisargadatta said: "One in a million will listen, understand and abide by the advice of the Guru, that ‘you are everything.’ He or she accepts with conviction ... [but] in most cases, the beingness assumes that it is a body that has taken shape, so one believes that he or she is born and will die. ... there is no death and no birth; one can never be born and die."

As long as there's a belief in an individual, BE that "one in a million! You are much closer to "the end" than “you" think. This that You are is closer than your breath. Notice that right now.

This is EVERYTHING ... and that's both inescapable and unimaginable.

37. There Is Really No "you" or "me"

S.P. Writes, *Came across your postings on the net accidentally/ spontaneously as everything happens. It is indeed a joy to see the clarity of the pointers from your talks. There is clear seeing of your message right here and now. There is really no "me". Hence, no questions or doubts arise. The seeing became clear recently for this pseudo-entity without any effort at all. Even the clarity of the Truth happens and not because some false entity called "me" wants it.*

Everything happens and all one can do is to have an earnest desire to know the Truth (like Nisargadatta Maharaj said). Till then it is only an intellectual battle for the mind; the mind that does not want to lose itself.

This email writing is happening like everything else. One can only point out the Truth as you are doing repeatedly but only a few will be able to clearly SEE the message (and not just understand it intellectually!).

This email is coming to you from another pseudo-entity who resides in the Midwest. There is no distance that can really separate us. There is really no "you" or "me". I am your own Self. Salutations and hopefully more will be able to SEE what you point to.

Onederful!

'Nuff Said!

38. You Are never NOT "Home"

Q: I found you on YOUTUBE. *I enjoy your teachings so much. I woke up for one day after listening to your 'I AM, STOP!" But next morning I was back in* LAH-LAH *Land. But being in the NOW for the short period was awesome. It felt so natural, so ordinary...I was home."*

Where is this “I” that "woke one day?" Seek the source of that “I.” You will end up only with what IS … No Thing. That is what You are, so to speak. THAT is Emptiness, Being-Aliveness, beyond language, the unknowable Knower of the states of sleep, dream, and waking-dream of the “I.”

You are never NOT home. There are just false expectations that some "state" that inevitably passes will be "permanent." There will be no such thing; it's a myth propagated by teachers and books that seem to promise some such. The experience you describe happened in being-Awareness and THAT, Being-Awareness, is simply NEVER actually missing, just overlooked. It is what you are RIGHT NOW ... wherever you go here you are, whatever the clock says it's only now. ALL there IS is NOW. Here. Now-Here/Every-w-here. Just see that what's being pointed to is indescribable AND unavoidable.

39. You Are THAT... and That IS No Thing.

Q: Every night I just kind of fall into seeing that I am not, and what is, is seen. Yet every morning, even though I try really hard to maintain it (silly I know) I wake stupid and stay stupid for the rest of the day, until about 1 AM or so when the seeing phase comes. During the day I will try my hardest. I will sometimes stop what I am doing and lock myself in my closet, determined to see this, and of course, nothing is seen. "I" am carried away by thought. Then at night it seems to happen by itself. Why would this be? Seeing and not seeing, truth or not, are just more bullshit states, aren't they?

Where is the "I" emanating from?

What is all this story appearing IN?

Who is asking this? Where is the thinker telling a story of "I" this and "I" that?

Where IS this person you take yourself to be?

You are THAT Emptiness which IS and IS KNOWINGNESS.

There is nothing to find, nothing to "stay with." The pointer is YOU ARE THAT. THAT is Being, inescapable.

Emptiness. Just That. Being Absolute Fullness. Just That.

This is No thing. You cannot "find" no thing. You ARE Self-Fulfilling emptiness ... No Thing/Everything. The wrods fail yet point...

Read this one over: A FEW times...

"Through conversations with "Sailor" Bob Adamson and the pointers he shared, I came to see that I was not the person I took myself to be. In fact, the person I assumed that I was did not even exist, except as an assumption. The entity at the center of my world, the very self around which my mind and all of its problems, questions, doubts and issues revolved, was not and never had been present.

All of those conceptual difficulties simply evaporated due to having no central point of reference any longer. One of the first recognitions was a very clear knowing that the spiritual search that had lasted several decades was over. This was not because any particular goal had been attained, but because the seeker had disappeared.

With the dissolution of the "I am" as a valid concept, any other concept which I habitually attached to that concept, such as "I am this" or "I am that" was rendered null and void. "I" no longer existed as the person I assumed I was. This did not mean that I disappeared. Relatively speaking, nothing changed at all. Perceiving, thinking, feeling, experiencing — all of these things went on as before. The difference was that things were no longer referred to a self-center, because there was no self-center.

This made all the difference, for as "Sailor" Bob Adamson once told me, suffering is nothing more than self-centered thinking. Suffering is a result of the belief in the reality of the separate self. And without the cause, can you have the effects? With the self-center out of the picture, what was left? What was I? Clearly I was still there, but not as anything I had previously taken myself to be. I existed, but not as some "thing". A better statement would be that I was no thing, meaning nothing in particular. I was aware, yet not confined to any particular state of consciousness. In this non-conceptual recognition, my being was vast, empty, clear, present, aware, utterly untouched by appearances, yet intimately connected to them all, naturally and effortlessly present, inescapable, beyond doubt, fearless and free. The personal suffering that had gripped my mind for years, even during the years of being a spiritual "person", simply could not reformulate any longer. And, most incredibly, this turned out to be the natural state that had been present from the start, only unrecognized until Bob Adamson pointed this out and encouraged me to see the obvious." *-John Wheeler*

It is exactly the same "here" ... I exist but NOT as some "Thing." and THERE: You exist but NOT as some “thing.”

You are that EXACT Same No Thing ... that Existing-ness that IS.

Don't believe it! It's NOT a mental assertion! Keep looking.

Then what isn't? Isn't that what we're trying to see here?

WHO is “trying to see? Is this is still uninvestigated? There is NOTHING to see and NO-ONE to see that!

If you believe in a false person, keep looking for some such. You always come up with nothing. That is the THAT in the phrase I AM THAT.

YOU ARE THAT. No thing appearing as some thing and all that needs to happen is to hunt down the who that talks and wants and see that you can NOT find such a "one." Full Stop.

40. Done!

J.H. Writes, *Over the past few months it's become clear - The search is over. Suffering is dead.*

Nowhere to go.

Nothing to get.

No one to convince.

The ordinary miracle of every moment now and now and now.

I so appreciate the time you took to help me see That. Thank you!

Peace and Love my friend.

Nothing to get, no one to get that ... and nothing to add! You (Oneness) did it!

41. Who Is Saying, "I Am Afraid?"

A seeker writes, *"I Am Afraid."*

This is a lie: There IS Existence ... Being Itself. This Beingness gets translated in language as "I Am." That "says" "I am afraid." All that is false.

Even this I am as a thought-story is false; it's merely a belief in or assumption of a separate "me" ... and that "one" cannot be found.

Discovering THIS ... RE-Cognizing this directly ... ends the fear and the suffering right now.

I Am, the NON-conceptual Being-Awareness, alive and real, IS what You actually ARE. Seeing this, apperceiving this, the search for fearless peace ends in the empty fullness that eternally IS.

42. The False IS Insecure

Q: I found your site just a few days ago, and every time I go back I see/hear exactly what I need right then. I also like your style. I'm hoping you can help me to see through the story of my life.

To say this indicates that you already see the story AS a story! That's a great start in my view. Now see that the idea of "me"and "mine, and "my", is also a part of the story! THIS is LIFE happening, not "your" life or "my" life.

The biggest things that anchor my belief in me right now are the physical sensation of tightness in my body that I interpret as fear/anxiety (and that feels like the seat of ME), and the identification of myself as a seeker.

Yes, that is the insecure vulnerable sense of a separate self. It's inevitably at the core insecure! Why? It suspects it is a fake; an inauthentic identity that has been believed in innocence from around the age of two or three, but is now thanks to "Grace" or whatever you like to call the Energy of Truth that arises from out of nowhere, the belief is crumbling. And quite possibly, that fake feels threatened!

The "seeker" is born of pain and insecurity and dies in the fire of being, the Absolute, which arises as an Energy of Aliveness. All is happening IN Absolute Being … that is what is Real and That arrives as Raw Aliveness -- THAT removes the false, so to say. No one is doing that. It happens, as everything happens … all by itself!

That said, there *are* ways to look into all this that appear to be helpful along the way.

Today, for instance, the thought "I'm a bad person" came up, and I saw it arise out of nothing and saw that it was nothing, and it occurred to me that I could be saying I was a piece of cheese and it would have exactly as much validity.

Exactly. ANY word that follows "I AM" IS false. And ultimately it is seen that the I am itself must go (and does … just as naturally as a sunset.)

This made me laugh and cry and within a minute (I had a brief respite) my mind was asking, "Is this It?" (because laughing/crying often accompany "realization") and then, "Oh no, I screwed it up!" accompanied by that strong physical sensation of anxiety/fear, and then, "what a great story [about me]!" (which I have now told). Ultimately, I got pulled back into believing in me again. That's a pretty typical series of events.

WHO says? Who "got pulled?" Did your Being disappear? Did Awareness and Aliveness become any less Aware and Alive??

Intellectually, I understand the teaching (and that it isn't really a teaching), and that ultimately I have no control whatsoever over whether this so-called waking up will even occur here.

Drop the understanding in favor of direct looking and experiencing what you ARE... simply BEING. And, emphatically it is NOT that "you" have no control. It is ultimately that there IS no "you" or "I" anywhere! But that, when only <u>believed</u>, can cause tremendous suffering in and of itself. This is a point we should talk directly about. Clearing this is a crucial "step."

Note: I found out the hard way that simply reading a book or two and attending a few "satsangs" will not bring about Self-Knowledge. It seems that in the play of Consciousness, the dream life of a "separate person" apart from a world of a billion billion pieces, there must be direct interaction with a true friend, one who shares from direct understanding *and* experience of what is real and what is false. One who can point you toward Home "One to One." It's been that way since time began and there have (fortunately) always been those who see correctly and are willing to share with no agenda. So do find a teacher to work directly with, one you feel comfortable with and can trust.

43. I Am Tired Of Seeking, I Want Peace

J.K. Writes, *I happened on one of your delightful videos (as a response posted to one of another teacher) and was very intrigued by what you had to say. It sounded very much like a teaching of which I am currently a student. Are you familiar with A Course in Miracles? How does it compare with what you are saying?*

Stay with the simple beginning pointer of that Course: Nothing Real can be threatened. Nothing unreal exists.

Forget the Course stuff about "God." God is only a concept, nothing substantial or real whatsoever! Stay with That which is known and not only undeniable and inescapable but also totally Real ... The NON-Concept NON-Experience of I AM.

That I AM is your Reality and ONLY That is The Real. EVERYTHING else is a concept or experience, temporal and unlasting. What NEVER changes? I AM. Not "me" or "you:" Just I AM. Impersonally, Nothing Being Everything. This Impersonal I AM is the Real ... and all else is belief, concept, hearsay, all second-hand, and all ... false.

If you must have a concept to point to what is real, the NON-conceptual Being-Awareness, stay with the One True Pointer to That: I AM. Refuse to entertain any other thought but one: I AM. That Thou Art.

And drop all questions except the One Eternally Unanswered and Unanswerable Question: Who Am I? The only "answer?" Not That Not That!

I was particularly struck by your emphasis on not being so much a "seeker" as a finder. You seem to downplay the necessity of practice in self-realization. The Course is chock full of exercises, in fact one whole volume is dedicated to exercise.

There is NOTHING to "find" and NO-ONE to "find it."

So these practices can never deliver on the false promise of "enlightenment" because they reinforce the idea of a seeker who is trying to find something that isn't already here now eternally. In short, you CANNOT "become" what you already ARE ... Being-Awareness-Aliveness.

Seeking is a sure-fire way to keep that from being seen.

However, the Course repeatedly says that the notion of a "process" is illusion and that enlightenment (the course calls it right-mindedness) could be achieved instantaneously.

There is NO such thing as enlightenment! And WHO would achieve some such mythical state? WHO? Do you know you exist? Yes. That I AM of Existence Itself IS what is REAL... So, there is NO such "state" as enlightenment and the appreciation of that brute fact is in itself the only enlightenment needed, as Nisargadatta Maharaj pointed out! And where is this "mind" that will get "right!?" That is a perfect and divine load of crap, dear One. LOOK: No-one ever gets "enlightenment." You are NOT gonna be the first! ☺ Why? Because there is NO "you" apart from the Whole.

This "me-myself-I" is nothing but an insubstantial and fleeting thought-feeling sense of a contracted energy that takes itself to be apart from the Whole, in ignorant arrogance. The word ignorance simply points to the IGNORING of the fact that Being IS. You are and that is absolutely known, by no-one. Arrogance is to ignore that we are ignorant and profess some ideal of a mythical state of eternal "personal peace of mind" or some other "spiritual snake oil."

I was wondering what were your thoughts on this? Thank you again for the videos and the website.

You're quite welcome, and lets be clear .... this expression is not "my doing." There are no teachers or students, paths or goals, in This I AM. It is what's happening (apparently) ... as Nothing being Everything... so ..... all there is is Being arising as all this expression and sharing.

I'm tired of seeking...I want to find...I'm tired of suffering...I want peace.

Yes, I recognize that. And the pointer is: There it is ... the Root Cause of Suffering ... right here in plain sight! ... This idea of a real separate solid entity called "I" .... when believed to be solid and real ... is the only (apparent) obscuration to this Being-Awareness … the belief in a separate "I" that "seeks and never ever finds…" that "I" is a false entity that appears real only due to ignorance and inadvertence.

Read the other dialogues on the website and in this book for more pointers regarding this. For now suffice to say that this "I" that seeks IS the apparent obscuration of Impersonal being-Awareness … and yet (Paradoxically) THAT TOO is Being-Awareness-Aliveness.

This seeming contraction of the energy-intelligence of Aliveness Itself into a little self-center we know as "me" or "I" is a happening of Being and is never apart from Being. What could ever be apart from Wholeness? The perfection of the dance of Being-Aliveness is this mystery of apparent separateness. But it's all imagination … a waking dream! See the dream AS a dream and then no-one wakes up to Being Nothing Being Everything and that means …. EVERYTHING.

Stay in touch till this is clear and there is no one left to practice or seek.

Then the Final Answer arises:

I Am - and That is Nothing Being Everything.

44. Peace Is Unknowing

Follow-up from J.K. - *Thanks so much for the detailed and impassioned response. I read and mulled over what you said last night. This morning, I listened to the dialogue that you sent me.* [a consulting call with Henryk; to request a copy write to Charlie and mention Henryk, at non.duality@yahoo.com].

I was struck suddenly by the apparent struggle the gentleman was having trying to understand the teaching. Something you said or inferred during the dialogue sparked a thought...it was, "Relax...there is nothing to know!" I immediately felt a great deal of peace, as if a huge burden had been lifted off my shoulders. I could hear myself in that gentleman...that was me trying to understand what is fundamentally not knowable. Everything and nothing is not knowable...so just smile! Dare I say it, even the I AM is just a concept...it simply is what is left after all concepts have been stripped away.

Conceptually ... correct! :-)

Am I pointing in the right direction?

YES.

And, as you know, there is NO "I" and NO "direction." Before This or anything is, Being IS or YOU ARE. (The NON-Conceptual Unknowable YOU.)

Be That and Nothing Else.

Part Three:

The Seeming “Process” From Arrogance to Freedom, “Take Two”

45. Seeing This Is not A Mental Conviction

G.B. asks, *So what was it that convinced you beyond the shadow of a doubt that consciousness was running the whole show and that there were no separate individual i's running around?*

The question contains a false premise. The assumption is that there is a “you” called Charlie that "got convinced."

Investigation happened. Inquiry into the false sometimes (no promises!) reveals it as false ... what thinks? What wants to know? And this so happened to show that the “me” that wanted to “be convinced” had no existence in reality. It was merely a thought, only taken on board as a separate “entity” called “me” due to ignorance ... ignoring the fact that there is NO evidence whatsoever for the existence of any separate entities anywhere, not here, not anywhere else!

But, it APPEARS that LOTS of “individuals” are running around. Just seeing the dream as a dream can happen. The dream of "an individual" appears separate and real. That’s the magic show! I watched Magician David Copperfield disappear a train locomotive! It’s absolutely convincing.

Who is it you believe is here that is convinced? There ain’t no such and the idea that there is a person there asking a person here is the cause of all problems. It can be seen through, but NOT by YOU! This seeing is the unquestionable absence of that which asks the question. This seeing is NOT a matter of conviction. It’s the absence of belief in either a person or conviction. The investigation itself is simply a movement of Energy – patterning as all there is; all that is happening, is One-Energy manifesting as This.

As-It-Is.

To tell a story, this investigation was apparently prompted in meetings with John Wheeler and 'Sailor' Bob, and others ... notably Tony Parsons, Annette Nibley and John Greven. But as we've discussed, as the "crow and coconut" metaphor points to; all notions of cause and effect are a story the mind tells itself to explain Life away:

A crow alights on a coconut tree and that very moment the ripe coconut falls on the ground. The two events are apparently related, yet the crow never intended the coconut to fall nor did the coconut fall because the crow sat on the tree. The intellect mistakes the two events as related, though in reality they are not. All of creation is the play of consciousness. As an unenlightened person may have a desire for action, and then perceives themselves doing action, the two are unrelated as the crow and the coconut. Consciousness is the actor, the action, the process and the witness of action. - Vasishta's Yoga

The mind is terrified by the idea that it has ZERO power to cause and control life. See that this mental questioning ... and all the usual seeker-guru posturing ... is simply an escape mechanism. It's a clever strategy to avoid confronting the absence of the so-called person who has any free will or independent ability to choose or decide, that avoids inquiry like the plague, out of fear for its (illusory) survival.

And, by the way, one subtle way "it" strategizes is to pretend "it" "now knows who it is!" That's a wild wooly madness indeed.

In actuality there is what is, exactly only happening as it is. Period. Full stop! No doer, only Life ... Life-ING. You are that experiencing, that Energetic Silence that keeps the stars apparently apart... Totality is Not Two. It is. This is IT. There are no hidden meanings or attainments or realizations to be had.

No one to be convinced! Full stop.

Have a beer!

Follow-up: *Mainly what was it that detached you from your identification with the I thought as a thing and revealed your true being?*

The question, like the first one, has a false premise. The false assumption is that there is in your words, a “you” (called “charlie”) that got detached from a false identity.
Look at this. A false entity! Who or what “gets detached from” some thing that has no real existence? This is chasing a phantom with a phantom. Waking up out of that happens, or it doesn’t. There can be investigation. There can be seeing the false as false. But there is NO "cause and effect" apart from a story (a tale told by an idiot signifying nothing.)

I have a "friend" in Georgia who says there is no cause and effect and that that is the answer, that there is no cause and effect. What say you?

Who cares? Who asks? Who says? Who is speaking and who is listening? I suggest that rather than look at what others claim as understanding, you find your own pathless way Home. Investigation seems to be key for most seekers.... and NO answer is "IT!"

In this final seeing there are NO ANSWERS! Drop all answers!. Try on simply NOT KNOWING. When it dawned that all my knowledge was actually ignorance, this got real clear. Really! ... the end game begins in not knowing a thing. Be in unknowing awareness. Just be. Just be. What never changes? Concepts change. Feelings change. Experiences change. Knowledge changes. Answers change. Beliefs come and go. What never comes and goes? What is always so, what does not sleep, does not wake, does not know, and yet IS?

Rather than compare pointers and get all wrapped up in this or that concept, seeking the "true concept," just recognize that all this is absolutely futile. The truth when spoken immediately turns to crap. Deal words, all lies! There is NO "Truth." There is only What IS.

There is no attainment, no realization, no enlightenment, no personal state of endless peace, nothing like that exists. What you are is beyond all this. Inconceivable, un-experienced and un-experienceable, nothing that can be known, said, conceived period full stop!

Q: And how long is a moment?

Okay, where does a "moment" start? Here? Now? When does "now" begin? When is it not now? Where is it not here? All this is merely the story of a "me" that "wants to know..." Who or what IS that "me?" Can you find one anywhere anywhen? What is always Present PRIOR to "Now?" Where is Awareness BEFORE there is "HERE?"

Without a thought, do you still exist? what is THAT??

What Never Changes?

What IS? Is there is Aliveness- Energy-Appearing-As This, "momenting" in (apparent time")??

46. Stubborn IS as Stubborn Does

G.B. Follows up: *In your book ["From I Am to I Am, With Love"] you state;"Know that you are presence awareness. Know that you are not a separate "person", also "Do you doubt that you exist? And...that you are aware? No one can deny the fact of his or her own existence." Who is this "you" that you constantly refer to?*

That separate personal "you" which you believe yourself to be.

Who is to say that the you that is referred to in my previous e-mail (see above and immediately below) is not the same you that you yourself refer to in your book?

You do. Or not. As a false entity claiming to be you.

As to your question "who is it you believe is here that got convinced?" Absolutely nobody, the question was purely self to self, I asked myself and believed that a straightforward answer would be the reply.

The reply as it always does bubbled up from nowhere and was in response to the energy that propelled the question ... the sense of a false entity asking. Then "you" the person did not like the reply. That IS the false "you," judging and evaluating. Who says what is "straightforward?" Only a judging mind-ego. The false "you" that asks and likes or doesn't like what is offered out of nowhere to no one, heart to heart, from I am to I am. At no charge, I would add. There was no agenda, no money requested, and no attempts made to sell anyone anything here.

If all my questions are coming from the false assumption that there is a me and nothing can be seen through by "me" then to whom are you addressing the statements in your book?

Asked and answered above. That stubbornness will make you suffer eventually, if it is not presently! I have some direct experience of that! It's not funny, and not pleasant. To say it straight, as a friend in England notes, "I hope you die soon." (The FALSE "you." What you are cannot die, That was never born!)

I never claimed enlightenment, so why is it that my questions are seen any different than those questions posed by those around me?

Ah, but you certainly did when you came to a meeting here, your demeanor and speaking indicated to everyone here that you were convinced that "you had gotten it" and you attempted several times to "take over and teach."But in any event, who said your questions are seen as different? Not I.

Look, dear One, NO answer is "IT!" This is as much a reference to that "friend" who made a claim the he or she had "the answer" as to the false "you" who has quoted the sage Sri Ramana Maharshi to me and seemed to be making a claim to the "final understanding." But look, WHO CARES? Only an ego, only a false self center, would give a hoot what was said in an e-mail? WHO or WHAT took that personally!!?? Find OUT!

Why are my questions seen as coming from some one who "claims they are no longer seeking and yet keep asking questions like this" as if my so called inquiry is not as genuine and authentic as the inquiry you yourself claimed to have done. If you see me as mis-representing myself I would ask you who it is that sees this?

Here you go again. Can you drop this and just BE what you are? No. Because you have NO control over this posturing and constantly trying to show that "you know."

Been there, suffered in that. There is compassion here, but no tolerance for arguments that are all about your own bullshit.

Look: Are you suffering? Get real with this. Rather than make all these accusations and couch all your "know-it-all-ness" in "questions," dig down and find out who the hell you are that wants to know and wants to be wise and clever!

If you see me as someone who "claims they are no longer a seeker" I never purported such, otherwise why do you think I attend satsangs?

I answered this already. But look: Who cares? All your righteous argumentativeness is NOT going to allow the natural freedom to be seen. WHO is this who "attends satsangs?" And may I remind you again that you did indicate more than once that you were not a seeker, just liked being with "like minded people?" That was also a dead giveaway, whether "you" know it or not! Just for clarity here, "I" do not see "you" as anything at all. It's all a show arising in Presence Awareness ... appearing as all this dance ... a dance of Intelligence, Energy, seemingly real, while what You are hides in plain sight from "you."

From my "understanding" there is "I" as a concept of a separate entity, which is how most people see themselves, isolated, cut off from that which is, that everything is separate, most people never even conceive of a universal I that is not a thought. Most people believe that what I points to is a body, even Ramana has said that this is the mis-identification, I associated with a body/mind,a thing instead of I seen as subject.

That may all be so, but so what? Drop it all! This intellectual understanding is the booby prize. It's another load of concepts. Quit spouting all that and LOOK for the one who "knows" all that garbage. And who and where are these "most people?"

It's all a story! YOU are not a story, nor a character, nor do you know what is real, and you never will know Oneness this way.

My questions are genuine, and I guess the answers that are expected go beyond the intellect, as I stated before when I went to my first satsang I knew that what was being said was true but did not know how I knew.

Look! Nothing is "true." You are believing concepts rather than LOOKING. WHO is this "I" claiming it knows? And again there is the judging mind and its expectations. Your expectations will never ever be fulfilled. Not here, not anywhere! WHO says there is any saying that is TRUE! There is NO such thing as a "said truth!" In ignorance we accept concepts as true and fail to notice the backdrop of pure non-dual Silence that these concepts arise within. And as to all knowing, ALL your "knowing" is actually ignorance. The so-called "truth" is found only when there is absolute NOT knowing. You have only gone from conceptual chains of iron to chains of gold.

Now I can say this,that perhaps you have not yet found an "outer teacher" who points out the Reality in a way that resonates for you. There are many fine teachers on my links page. For your personality, I suspect that Annette Nibley might be helpful to you. Go explore, until the suffering is ended.

As for myself I refuse to "parrot" intellectual knowledge, as it has been said "you know it like spit in the mouth" that's when it's genuine.

This is funny! After parroting Ramana Maharshi you make this claim! All this is is yet another concept! Are you FREE? Or are you suffering? Get real, get with the direct and uncompromising pointing, get down off your high horse! It's YOUR suffering. I could care less whether you are a parrot or not or what judgments the mind you believe is you makes. If my pointing isn't resonating find someone else, for your own sake, dear One.

*All answers are conceptual, it's the space they come from which defines th*em.

More bullshit. Dear One: Ultimately, there ain't no defining and ain't no space and ain't no "comes from." All there is is this Energy-Aliveness, appearing. You are simply stuck in identification with the mind. Wake up out of this intellectual story and see what is real, the NONCONCEPTUAL overlooked spaceless timeless Isness of Aliveness.

And yes there is still a seeming appearance of a separate entity here, as is stated there is nothing that cause's the effect of the disappearance of the belief in a separate entity, or as Ramana states it, it is like a burnt rope, it still has the appearance of a rope but no longer has the power to bind.

That sounds very wise but you cannot have it both ways. If there is truly seeing that the I is an appearance only and that it's like a burned rope, then WHY do you fight and argue and ask ask ask all these questions? The stubbornness disproves what you say, over and over. No person no fight no blame. Throw away all your books and wise sayings and get down and get real. Go find a teacher you can work with who will not buy your bullshit and who you can respect. Your disrespect for the space here is palpable and unwelcome; it benefits no one to argue and fight for concepts and beliefs!

I stand by this from my website: "Perhaps the habit is to identify your self as the thought "I" - as in I Am. Notice right now if the Presence behind the I thought has been overlooked. Break into the habit, being aware of That Presence as your True Identity. This takes no time nor practice. It's just a natural seeing ...

right here, right now. And that's the end of seeking; the Natural, Eternal Stateless Being has been found to be never missing".

And this, from Seng Ts'an, in The Hsin Hsin Ming...

"Don't waste time in doubts and arguments that have nothing to do with this. One thing, all things, move among and intermingle without distinction. To live in this realization is to be without anxiety about non-perfection. To live in this faith is the road to non-duality, because the non-dual is one with the trusting mind."

"Words!The Way is beyond language,
for in it there is no yesterday
no tomorrow
no today."

If it is heard heart to heart then all is said and done. if not? That's okay too. Go to satsangs. Pretend to be a non-seeker spiritual enlightened person. Enjoy the dance. See a film. Have some fun! Over and out.

47. The Tirades of the Mind

(And All This Arises IN the Unbounded Presence-Awareness That You ARE!)

D. R. Writes, *This is what I can't quite grasp: terms liked "consciousness" and "awareness" get tossed around a lot. One of the questions that that you ask people to ask themselves is "Do I exist?" It seems the answer is yes, based on the premise that you cannot deny you are aware; conscious.*

The pointer is that Awareness IS; Existence IS. Being IS. These are all just LABELS: NO label will ever be accurate! You see, That which is being pointed to is both undeniable, AND ungraspable by the split-mind of "I/Other." So: Existence-Awareness IS; what you call you is a thought-form that seems (only seems!) to be an energetic contraction, a self-center called "me," that feels as if it exists apart from That … yet this energy of "I" is NEVER actually separate or apart from That. Awareness is what you are; you don't "own" Awareness, you ARE Being-Awareness, Consciousness, Lovingness! (Sat-Chit-Ananda in Sanskrit, the ancient sages' language) ... and ONLY That…you are NOT "a" being. You are Being, One-Without-A-Second. Being Nothing, Being Everything, Being all in between! NOT Two...

But if you have ever been under anesthesia during major surgery, you are not conscious. You are not aware. It is essentially like awareness or consciousness ceases to exist until you wake up. What is going on here?

This is a confusion of terms, and what seems to be missing is a distinction, subtle yet crucial, between Consciousness (the knowing Presence that the mind labels as I AM) … and the A Priori Being-Awareness (NO THING.) Being, Awareness ItSelf As-It-Is, IS Eternally PRIOR to Consciousness OF presence......

that Consciousness which awakes and appears as "you" … the "I Am" of Being-Consciousness-Awakeness.) Simply: Being is PRIOR to and BEYOND Consciousness yet NOT APART from Consciousness. They are of One-Essence, One-Taste. One-Not-Two. NON-duality! Like one taste of the ocean and the whole ocean is known....

What beats the heart and breathes air into and out of the lungs of that organism during the absence of consciousness under anesthesia? THAT is what is often labeled as Awareness. Actually I find a more resonant pointing-label to be ALIVENESS. This Being-Aliveness (another label I like) is That Energy-Intelligence or Essence of Aliveness ItSelf, which "Lives" the body when there is NO Consciousness. The mind simply CANNOT grasp This Presence itself. The mind is an appearance IN This Presence. The eye cannot see itself.

Just see this right now! This Being-Aliveness that IS, the REAL YOU, actually always IS and THAT arises AS Consciousness, which gets translated by the dividing energy of "mind" into the conceptual believed-in "entity" called "I Am." THE TRUE I AM is Being-Awareness-Aliveness, which is Existence Itself, and never absent. THAT is what is ever-present, EVEN in deep sleep or under anesthesia.

This is a very good question: I had a similar one, since in the story (only the story!) of this bodymind machine, it was under anesthesia for over six hours for quadruple bypass open heart surgery in 2000. The resolution came when it got clear for no-one that the blankness of that "time" was the true nature of Being-Aliveness. ALL else is imagination.

Now the question I have for you is, are you suffering? Let's get at THAT. Ask you the question - do you exist? That produces the immediate "knowing" of the pure I AM of Consciousness.

Then the *thought* "I Am" is the LABEL the mind uses to separate itself from the Whole (apparently, not actually...)

Then WHAT or WHERE are "you?" What IS this "I AM" and where is IT located? Find the Source of That "I AM" ... if you can! Then it may be seen, again, by no-one, that what You are is this Being-Aliveness Energy, boundless and free.

Staying with the inescapable yes-ness of your very Being Itself, looking into Empty Naked Awareness from Empty Naked Awareness ... so long as "you" are believed-in as an "entity" you can put that apparent one to the task of discovering what is REAL and what is NOT REAL. ONLY the Real never changes, even in deep sleep or under anesthesia! And nothing UNREAL actually exists. It was all a dream-story. Imagination. Find this out and suffering is over and done forever. And, "staying with" the actuality of Being is the easiest of all: YOU ARE That and cannot escape That! Consider these two pointers From John Greven:

"Stay with that which lovingly allows for everything to appear in peace that cannot be disturbed. Allow that to show you the depth of its void and the fullness of its emptiness."

And, "The Supreme Subject is unattainable, unimaginable, undeniable, ever present, and manifest as the thought 'I Am'. Seek The Source of 'I Am'."

Stay in touch until the questions (and the questioner) are dissolved back into that Eternal Being-Awareness that you truly are.

48. Mind Resisting Being Seen as A Fake

Follow-up from D.R. - *Is it possible that a conversation could take place that does not revolve around the analysis and deconstruction of every word and concept "D.R." says or "D.R." uses? Yes, "I" was GONE under anesthesia. "I" wasn't there. Yes, yes, yes. The term "I" and the word "experienced" is used for a lack of a better word. How else can "I" say it? Give me a break already. It's pissing me off already. If I can predict what you are going to say in response, would it no longer be necessary for you to give that response? Well OK D.R., who is this D.R. that is pissed? Where is this pissed D.R.? Can you locate the D.R. that appears to be pissed? Who is this me that is supposedly D.R. that is supposedly pissed? Me, Me, Me.....Who is this me?? Who is D.R.? IS D.R.? IS? Is there no small respite from the ranting and raving, my friend?? Just humor me for a minute. Please. We have a body, the body lives, then the body dies. Awareness and consciousness are more or less present when the body lives. Do awareness and consciousness cease when the body dies, even though being-aliveness always IS? Or am I just wasting my time (again) asking a stupid, apparently ignorant question which is going to elicit yet another bull-shit-laden and evasive response*?

Yes, "you" are pissed. Because "you" do NOT want to discover that "you" are a phantom: This "you" that you "know yourself to be" does not actually exist!

You are not listening. You waste your time arguing with no one! So, dear One, you need to find another to share with that you can resonate with. Best of luck, and I sincerely hope "you" die soon. Until "you" are seen to be false there will be suffering and pissed-off-ed-ness. So it is… and, LOVE says, I AM loves You so I AM is out to destroy "you".

49. More Tirades of the Mind

More Follow-up from D.R. - *Am I not listening? Or are you just a cop out? You tell me essentially to go away because you don't want to deal with me. I'm just a non-listening, ignorant, suffering pain in the ass. Wasting my time or wasting your time, old man? But then you decide to try yet again to get me to "listen" a few hours later with your "you" analysis!*

Maybe I am not listening because what "you" are "saying" is crap. Maybe what I don't want to "hear" is YOUR CRAP. Maybe you you've got other people who are like, "Charlie, thanks so much for your help! You've helped me so much Charlie! Wow, Charlie, you have helped me so much! Thank goodness for Charlie!"

Are those people who "resonate" with Charlie who Charlie helped so much no longer suffering??? Did you even really help them???? It's nice thought, though, isn't it. If they tell you, "wow, you helped so much, Charlie," what, then they resonate with you? Let's continue a dialog with those people because THEY MUST be listening where D.R. is NOT! They hear! But D.R. does not! Let's stay in touch with those ingratiating, beautiful people! Especially that 22 year old who is clinically obsessed with enlightenment! But then "D.R." come along and says you are a pain in the ass to talk to Charlie and you are full of crap Charlie and you are like you are arguing with no one! We are not resonating! Go find some one else! GO AWAY, D.R.!

What? You don't like my ranting and raving? You don't like your own medicine, Charlie??

I do resonate with some one else. The interactions are sweet and loving and very respectful blah blah blah. It's true! This is some one who single-handedly destroyed my "reincarnation-past-life-karma" bull-shit belief system cherished and clung to for dear life for over 25 years in about 5 minutes flat!! (Wait, you mean you have some "resonating" people you correspond with out there who still believe that shit?? They still believe in Santa Claus?? And they are ready to "hear" Charlie, but D.R. is not?? Holy shit!!) I was like, yes, I hear you. No anger. No freaking out. Just, "OK, it is what it is. OK"

You are some "one on the side." It's like when you are dating some one, then you might have a few you see "on the side." Just for the hell of it. I like you, although you might not understand that and may not be able to stand me, by now. I like arguing with non one. It is what it is. I argue because I am trying to figure something out. Telling me to stop figuring things out isn't going to make me stop. It will stop when it stops, right? Can I really control the stopping of my imaginary mind? Can I? But if there is no one to argue with, I won't argue any more.....there's nothing to stop, is there?

Yes, wow, that's some truly wonderful mind-stuff! The endless Tirades of Mind; fascinating to observe arising from Nothing, ranting a while, and disappearing back into Nothing. What great fun! Good on ya, D.R..

I love you.

PS: *You asked, "when you die, is the experience of death, in essence, the same as when you are under surgical anesthesia?"*

TRUE answer? I don't know. Who knows that? Isn't THAT, as Shakespeare said ... "That undiscovered country from whose bourne no traveler returns..." ??? To me, it's clear as day that what I AM and what YOU ARE is Unborn Timeless Being. Clueless Nothingness.

So that's what there was an attempt to point to, as your background with another teacher was not expressed and I took you to be a "seeker." I am happy you are not suffering and you already found someone to point things out in ways that worked for you.

Anyhow, I love you. Have a beer and some chips, on me.

PPS: Didn't you NOTICE? This is merely an overlooking of The ever-fresh Obviousness of Being Itself, and speculating and imagining a "you" that "was born and will die..." AND ...

ALL This Arises IN the Timeless Presence-Awareness that You ARE.

50. Clueless Nothingness

Yet another follow-up from D.R. who writes, *Me again.*

Dear "Seekers," there is nothing to seek. Nothing to discuss. Nothing to point to. NOTHING to point to. NOTHING TO POINT TO. All that is IS nothing. Less than nothing. Less than nothing to the 100th power. Less than nothing to the "infinite" power. Unimaginable nothing-ness IS....IS IS IS IS IS. "You" cannot "know" the nothingness which is being. "You" cannot "experience" the nothingness which is being. Yet "you" are "IT." There is no YOU. There is no IT. Sorry for all the bull-shit. Have a good life. Love, [D.R. calling herself] "Charlie" ... P.S. This website and all bull shit contained there-in will self destruct in: 10,9,8... PP.S When you're done with your inces-sant sniveling, see what IS. PPP.S There is no is. Sorry.

Hi "me"

Hey, the "bullshit" is aliveness, being bullshit, and so it is. Great fun, this dream of "me," ain't it dear One?

Love ya,

I AM

[appearing as D.R./Charlie]

51. The Ventriloquist's Dummy

D.R. strikes again! Criticizing a John Wheeler essay and the video wherein I share that, she says: *Consider THIS (or not) and feel free (or not) to share with those who email pure drivel to which I AM responds with equally hilarious tripe (I AM such a mean little shit! But I prefer the term Feisty ONE). Here IT IS:* "You" *are driving down the highway. Very suddenly IT IS 10 minutes later. 15, 20 minutes, what ever. What happened to those 10 or 15 minutes? "You" (who does not exist) doesn't remember the "lost" non-existent time. What happened to IT? Where did IT go? I have experienced this* .....

Blah blah blah, all about "I!" This "person" does not see that "experience" is NOT what is being pointed to! So this ignoramus continues for paragraph after paragraph of "enlightened-ego" bullshit. And as to those two "terms" she uses as her self-concept, I'm going with the first ... a "*mean little shit.*"

My response to her is: "Don't bother me with any more of your bullshit. Don't e-mail me again until you are sincere and are about ending your suffering. I'm done with you, lady. Piss off." That was sent last night and her e-mail address was put into the "twit filter."

"Sailor" Bob Adamson essentially told me get lost at one time, when I was being disrespectful and "egoing" on him trying to pass off some crap like like this, as D.R. is doing. THAT was wonderful! Like Nisargadatta before him, Bob is wonderfully REAL and nothing is filtered through some phony need to "be nice." The ones who have seen the falseness of the "egoic entity" and no longer give it any energy are not "careful!" They are, quite simply, authentic. Aliveness doesn't filter; only a mind-bound ignorant one such as D.R. would give a shit. And of course Bob never "gave up" on "me" in actuality. How could

One "give up" on One? So "later" there was much laughter about all that!

There is NO controlling "personal will" involved here, OR in “D.R.”; there is only Aliveness, and that includes any ignorant expression, and all the associated feelings and thoughts about that, and the “reaction” of “piss off!” and so on. Life living itself through rattlesnakes and Sailor Bobs. Yee ha! Rock on. This Peace that IS LOVES it all as it is. WHO does not see this?

The ventriloquist's dummy will NEVER "know" the ventriloquist.

"Stupid IS as stupid DOES" *(- the 'modern sage' Forrest Gump)*

But....

WHO CARES?

"Well, words are always in battle, they are dualistic... based on subject-object. It is possible to analyze everything that is said and expose the futility of verbal expression on this subject... but it is a shallow activity born of the frustration of not being able to sense where the words are pointing." - *Tony Parsons, writing in “Nothing Being Everything.*

You can get it at www.theopensecret.com.

52. Stay With The Simplicity Of This

D.R. Writes one more time ... finally getting real! *OK. I'm 100% finished with the bullshit. And I apologize for being a such hurtful little shit to you, Charlie (I saw the video). Thank you for your brutal honesty. I am sincere. I feel like I want to ask you something, but for once, I am at loss for words and not able to articulate well.*

Just stay with the simplicity:

1. You are Ordinary Being-Consciousness-Aliveness. Nothing special about that.

2. You are NOT <u>anything</u> but That.

53. Is There No End To Suffering?

More from D.R. Who sincerely asks, *I am simply ordinary being-conscious aliveness. OK, staying with this. But then the suffering continues. A while back you said to simply come back to I AM, but doing that simple thing, suffering is still there. The "end of suffering" - is this just another mind-concept illusion and in reality, there is no end to suffering?*

The root cause of all suffering is the belief in a "person," an "entity" with control or will to alter or modify or correct what is arising ... and looking into that can happen ... then it is seen (by no-one) that there IS no such "controlling entity" ...

The happening of that is NOT by will. Only Being arises as The One ... looking into itself nakedly ... examining the false to see it as false. Being IS. That Thou Art. Try to get away from being! Can't be done.

The person is false. That Thou Art NOT. Re-discover that and the search is over ... for no-one. This cannot be grasped or conceived. Let go of grasping, striving and comprehending this ... The final seeing is that ...

All there is is Being, and not even that.

What IS Is NOT. What Is NOT, IS. - *John Greven*

54. Waiting For a Shift? You'll Wait Forever

And a follow-up from D.R. - *As the un-concealing is happening, does this "me-ing and be-ing" stop, then, just awareness of spontaneous"be-ing" only? Or is just always like this, this awareness of "me-ing and be-ing?"*

There's a love of the sincerity and the "heart-born" inquiry happening there. I'm very glad to see the "righteous mind" taking a back seat. In so-called "awakening" there appears this "me-ing and be-ing." In so-called "liberation" there is no movement appearing. But BOTH of these are happening IN Being-Awareness. This True Eternal State-less-ness is never missing and cannot "come and go" as what seems to be the case in this "me-ing and being." That is a pointer, a conceptual story about a description of something that is appearing IN Timeless Spaceless Relationless BEING-AWARENESS.

Can Awareness be more or less awareness? Can Presence be more or less Presence"? Being-Awareness IS and you are That. Everything is appearing IN That. In Truth there is no "spontaneous be-ing." That is an experience and no experience is "it." This notion of "me-ing and being" is a fair pointer but when it becomes a "truth" it is just dead! Then it becomes something along the lines of a philosophical description; and can give rise to a cul-de-sac speculation about some "time when" there "will be" a "shift." It's quite common to caught out by that pitfall. There is ONLY ALWAYS Being-Awareness. And "always" is not just "a long time!" It's Timeless, Eternal.. So a giving up of this "trying to grasp and understand" may or may not happen, and Being-Awareness shines freshly on and as that happening as well. All is happening spontaneously all the "time" anyway. ALL. And there IS only The IS of Being-Awareness.

You are Unborn Perfect Freedom. ALL else is appearance in and on that, and impermanent. All is well in The Unconceieved Unperceived Unimaginable Ever-Fresh Unborn. Don't trade the

Unborn Being-Awareness for these paltry thoughts or stories, or any beliefs or philosophical concepts.

I saw the latest video - something caught the attention - talking about the interim sense of I can control making my coffee, etc, but not able to control the unfolding of life....when in the awareness of being which has been going on, noticing there is a sense of no control at all over anything at all - the hand is grabbing the towel, etc., like the body is a puppet, as described below...

Sure. And that is all happening IN what you are ... Being-Awareness, appearing as Timeless Presence and Full Blown Aliveness! ALL is included in ALL!

... so the false mind is just crazy idiot wanting to know this and that! Trying to make sense of this coffee comment!

Be with the energy rather than trying to make sense of it. Yes, the mind IS the storytelling crazed fool, telling the false story of a suffering "me" ... it is the "tale told by an idiot, filled with sound and fury, signifying .... nothing!"

Does the me-ing ever fully "die??"

The "me-ing" is a function of the organism. There is NO suffering in the idea of a functional me that can make coffee. The suffering consists in the belief in a psychological ego-me that "should be able to control feelings emotions thoughts etc." is somehow real. Seeing the false as false, the organism is still being lived by Being-Awareness (so to say) and this certainly includes the <u>functioning</u> aspect of "mind." But there is no longer a belief that whatever appears ought to be better or different or that "someday" there will be "more nothing" or "less me." This is IT. This is all there is to "get" ... as Nisargadatta said, "There is no enlightenment. Appreciation of this fact is itself 'enlightenment'."

This is it. Full Stop.

55. Accept-ing With No Accept-er

D.R. Checks in - *It has been several weeks since the so-called "awakening." There appears to be a interesting phenomenon happening: there is an ever present sense of NOT caring one way or the other any more about whether there is this going back and forth between so-called "bondage/duality" and so-called "liberation/oneness." This appearance of movement between me-ing and be-ing appears to be happening always and may never appear to stop. Or it may. Who the hell cares. There is no desire to seek a way out of this sense of back and forth. One might say, there is just acceptance of what is. Allowing for what is.*

Like the empty sky, Awareness is always ever-fresh and allowing anything and everything to appear and dissolve while remaining untouched and eternally free…

Well then must have slipped into the "being" phase again while writing that last bit there (!)

That is all beautifully articulated. Steady wisdom ... accept-ance with no accept-er.

56. Who Cares? There's No One TO Care

Final Follow-up from D.R. – *I've heard this so-called"phenomenon" referred to as "non-dualistic wobbling" (as in "wobbling" between what appears to be duality and non-duality) in some "metaphysical" circles, which apparently does not in any manner "diminish" the "realization" of the "realized one."..... not that this one really gives a crap about said "phenomenon!!" ....What a load of FUN crap....*

Fun indeed! Being everything ... what a wild ride.

Welcome To The Home You never Actually Left!

Part Four: Conversations With No-One About Nothing

57. Do You Exist?

Z.S., a reader of “From I Am To I Am, With Love,” Writes, *There is an openness time to time. However, when I wake up there is this dullness once again and when I ask myself, 'do I exist?', as absurd as it may sound, I feel like I don't exist! Its like my mind is against the idea. 'I' do know there is no 'I' intellectually but it just hasn't dawned at a gut level. The hardest part for me is the sense of being in my heart.*

This is returning you to the FACT that there is NO person. You ARE and that is clear and obvious at all times. Asking do I exist reveals that you DO exist but NOT as a "separate knowable thing" called "me myself and I!"

This is very good news. Don't fight this; let that Emptiness show you the Infinite Fullness of Self-Loving Being. THIS is Aliveness with no "person" claiming ownership. Life Itself and THAT is the Real. Good work; keep at it, Z. That sense of being is okay, that's how the organism is able to function. It is only when you take that sense of being SEPARATE that suffering kicks in.

Don't wait for it to dawn. It will happen without your efforts! Why? Because there is NO controlling person in there anywhere and once that is glimpsed the mind-stuff might "play out" this way but you are really "done for" as far as "mistaken identity" goes.

Again, just keep going. You are doing great.

58. Does Awareness Care? WHO cares?

AJ writes, While watching one of your videos I heard you say: 'I am interested in ending your suffering'. This kind of struck me and so the following question arose: Does Awareness care? Who cares???Is it nonconditional Love with a capital L that cares? Who's the one that's interested??? Would you please elaborate on this. Lots of Love and a warm hug from a Dutch friend!!!!

This is an excellent question!

This caring "happens." Nobody cares: This is the happening of nobody caring. Through some organisms there is apparent caring or empathy i.e. Mother Teresa or "sailor" Bob Adamson or John Wheeler or Stephen Wingate. Through some organisms there is NO apparent caring, NO empathy... i.e. Saddam Hussein or Charles Manson ... OR even some VERY direct no-bull Nonduality "teachers" (Wayne Liquorman comes to mind, no disrespect, just how it appears "here.") But LOOK! On investigation it is seen ... there is no "person," no "entity" DOING or CREATING this naturally arising "caring."

So when the expression comes out, regarding a caring about ending your suffering, that is simply Oneness, appearing as This and Being That Caring.

"*Who is the 'one' that is 'interested'?*" No-One is interested. There is nothing and no-one caring about anything. THIS is what "no-one and nothing caring about anything" looks like! You see, the mind-brain machinery thinks of love as the opposite of hate. And it thinks of caring as a person caring, offering some pity or feeling-sorry-for. That is all bullshit. This LOVE (as you say with a Capital L) simply IS.

This Love, I call Aliveness (ALL LIVE-NESS), Isness, Being-Awareness, or Deliciously Inescapable Choiceless Cluelessness, or .... "Marmalade!"

Call it whatever, "it" (words! "IT" is not a thing, the word is a lie!... but words are what is happening here, so .....) "IT" (Livingness-Beingness) IS, and "IT" stands alone as Nothing and Everything. Aliveness equally loves BEING both love and hate, both war and peace, both caring and not caring, both Saddam and Teresa, ALL the "pairs of opposites." Being-Aliveness-Lovingness (Sat Chit Ananda) has NO Opposite expect in the story of "me and other-than-me." THIS is, as my dear friend Tony Parsons puts it, "Nothing Being Everything."

THIS Being-Aliveness is "IT." NOW: Where is any exclusion OR inclusion in THAT!??

Thanks for a really great question. It appears in the dream-story that lots of "seekers-on-the-edge" have been stuck in that one. And lots of love and a warm hug right back at-cha! Before All, During All, and After all, You ARE That Love. So Love says hello to Love and Love asks a question and Love answers a question. There is Only Love ... Being all of This ... Totality.

Aliveness. Only That.

59. "You" were Never Born

A.J. Writes again: *Sri Nisargadatta Maharaj says: "Knowing you are nothing is wisdom. Knowing you are everything is Love". This suggests there are two steps. One step is the realization: I am no-thing. Second step is the realization: I AM LOVE.*

A.J., I have one question for you, now: Are you suffering? All this philosophical meandering will never end the suffering of the seeker. You'll have a library full of quotes and pointers that you can read while you're suffering, OR you can look at what is Real and what is False and end the seeking and suffering right now. It seems that it's "up to you." But is anything up to this idea of a "you?"

1. Do you exist? YES, before thought is, you are this: I AM.

2. Who are you? Nothing but That. Ask YOU, "Who Am I?"

So long as there is a belief in a "you," a "doer," put that doer-you to the task of asking "Who Am I?" and ONLY THAT, until no "separate one" that believes he is and can do, is left to ask. "Who Am I?"

From listening to and watching the various expressions of non-duality-teachers I get the impression that most of those teachers only realized the first step. I am No-Thing. As I see it that looks like a DONUT. You know, donut, hole in the center, rest of the cake one perfect ZERO. The hole being the space where once the ego dwelled. The ZERO-shape can be seen as the remaining, persisting activity of what I call 'self-ing'. Consciousness has not ceased to be.

Pass the donuts, I'm hungry. I'll have a chocolate one! Look: Consciousness is an ASPECT of Being. Call that Being-Awareness or Being-Consciousness; words that POINT to the indescribable Eternal Isness of The Whole.

But first off let's get the Nisargadatta quote accurate: The above is an interpretation. That's what the mind does, and that's why the direct pointers of a Christ or a Buddha, a Ramana Maharshi or a Nisargadatta, are lost in the mire of reinterpretation by ignorant minds that altered the sayings to fit THEIR conceptual understanding. And the seeker suffers due to this misinterpretation! Here is as close as we can get (Maurice Freydam's translation, in "I Am That"): "When I know I am nothing; that is wisdom. When I know I am everything; that is love. My life moves between the two."

Leaving out the third pointer,"...life moves between the two," is what the mind does to separate wholeness. The inclusiveness of the whole quote is lost as the focus goes on two apparently separate occurrences.

Of course the word "when" implies "time" and so we always have a falling short of the actual whenever words are used. Words ONLY point to the Timeless Wordless Isness of The Natural Eternal Being-Presencing-Aliveness.

And so dear One, this myth of "steps" and "realizations" and "becoming" will keep the seeking mind stuck in the story of path and goal forever! The sudden Seeing is always right now and is spontaneously BOTH Nothing AND Everything ... and all there IS, is That Love, loving to BE. Full Stop. All that arises is arising IN You As You: Not Two. This word, "Advaita," is a description of an indescribable Seeing that all there is, is One-Essence, Aliveness. This cannot be repeated too often! So, this is the great death of paths and goals in what IS ... This Being. Nothing Being Everything, if you like.

All you are doing here is analyzing pointers. LOOK where the pointers POINT!

Tony Parsons says that after the 'walk in the park' there were many years of alternating 'me-ing' and 'be-ing'. This activity finally died away and ever since LOVE shines.

LOVE that embraces everything. The energy of the personal self has burnt up and no-self is the living reality. 'Gone, gone beyond' as the Buddha says. Nirvana! Beyond Being.

So that's a description of a story and when you take the story as a 'path" you stay stuck in becoming! There is NO "state" of "no-self, living reality." Again and again comes the pointless pointer: All there is, is this Aliveness, and THIS includes absolutely all of it, everything: THIS IS IT: This ... pain, pleasure, seeing, not seeing, apparent bondage, apparent liberation, being and not being ... WHAT can be EXCLUDED from the Whole!!?? THIS IS the "*LOVE that embraces everything!"* <u>It's never been ABSENT!</u> This mind delusion is of a "person" trying to grasp the Whole and the "person" is merely an idea in your mind. All you are seeing is your own mind, which ultimately is the One "minding" but in this interim dark night you believe it is real and so try to figure out how to not be!

So okay, go ahead, get away from Being. Run! Run fast and maybe you'll escape your Being-Awareness-Aliveness! RUN!

How's that going?

Getting stuck in the first step is getting stuck in what Tony calls 'The Glasshouse". A sort of getting frozen in space. This can be very delusive.

To WHO? You believe all this crap? Tony would be laughing his head off I suspect, at how you re-interpret what is being shared. This is YOUR delusion, no one else's, dear friend. The simplicity of The Message is not being heard, because "you" are "trying to hear it!"

One can have the notion of being enlightened. But underneath the self is subtly lurking in the dark. The final frontier is not yet passed. Is there a final step beyond Being? And is there a total cessation of consciousness? A total and absolute death before the dead of the body.

This death is what IS. "You" were simply never born! All that was born and can die is an idea, a fixated belief in a separate entity called "me" that believes it OWNS "this body" as "my" body" and these thoughts and feelings as "my thoughts and feelings" and this apparent universe as "my universe." But HOW can what was never ever born ever "die?" You are already dead. Dead man talking!

See that all that is happening is that a "me" identity is fixated on stories of paths and final steps and someday and perhaps there will be a dropping off of the false. Seemingly it dawns on "you" that there IS no "you" and there never WAS. But that will ever and only be Right Now Right Here … and since you are and you cannot escape that you are, Being Itself, then there may be a hearty laugh and then it's off to the pub!

How do you look at this Charlie? Does what I'm saying make sense or is it Bullshit?

It may "make sense" to a mind. BUT: All that "makes sense" is FALSE! Why trade the Unborn Aliveness for "understanding?" That's to sell a diamond for the price of spinach!

Again, A.J., I repeat the one question I have for you, now: Are you suffering? All this philosophical meandering will never end the suffering of the seeker. You'll have a library full of quotes and pointers that you can read while you're suffering, OR you can look at what is Real and what is False and end the seeking and suffering right now. It seems that it's "up to you." But is anything up to this idea of a "you?" Do you exist? Who are you?

~ ~ ~

Follow-up: *Thank you for your wonderful reply!*

De Nada! :-)

...my question came from reading the works of [names another writer]. I don't know if you are familiar with her writings?

Nope.

She wrote three books ... In these books she writes about a journey, a passage through consciousness (or self) and the gradual falling away of that, finally resulting in a total cessation of the human experience and the mysterious arising of Christ-Consciousness, which is -in her view- the same as the Buddhist 'Dharmakaya'. I have always regarded these writings as a monstrous piece of 'spiritual' bullshit, but still intriguing.

Intriguing to the mind only. Bullshit is nearly always interesting to a seeking mind because it thinks it's finding some answers to the I DON'T KNOW of Non-Conceptual Being-Awareness-Truth -- and the Mysterious Abyss is to be filled with concepts so that the mind-me entity which never was avoids it's own demise ... totally paradoxical and utterly ridiculous!

Especially where she throws up the possibility of a second step of going beyond 'the unitive state' as she calls the falling away of the I-thought. This is where the donuts come from. Her description of ego-less man. In your reply this is being exposed as total and utter bullshit, absolute phony baloney! THERE IS ONLY EVER THIS. FULL STOP!!!

Yep.

The simplicity of the message is obvious. There is NO-ONE. Period!!!! What Tony Parsons calls the 'Glass box' is a mind game, that's how I understand it. All mind games are illusions. Survival-games of holding on to the belief in a separate entity. Tony also often says: 'Having a clear understanding of this message doesn't mean there is liberation'. Now that's an interesting statement.

It has to do with leaving out Nisargadatta's third pointer "...life moves between the two".

Isn't it Charlie ? I really enjoy this communication. Going mad over THIS"!!!! WOW!!!!!!!

I say that this way: (I think Tony might also) -- "Understanding" Being-Awareness-Aliveness is NOT Being Being-Awareness-Aliveness.

Being-Awareness-Aliveness IS. The understander is a phantom, an idea appearing and disappearing IN Being-Awareness as a "facet" or "aspect" OF Being-Awareness. That's all there is to this clear seeing, which no-one sees and nobody knows.

This apperception ends the search, here and now, forever.

60. Much Fun in The Unborn!

Follow-up from A.J. - *You ask me: "Are you suffering?". The answer is: "I am not suffering !" You are right. All this philosophical meandering will - as far as the mind is concerned, go on for ever. I can go on reading another 10 billion books and still get nowhere. Here the seeking has ended for sure. The question: "Who am I???" got lost in infinity. There is no-one here!*

Do I exist? YES!

Who am I???? I don't know!!!!

That's all perfectly clear. Just like airplanes in your videos are happening, so is tapping these keys happening! This IS IT!!!!!!!

Exactly!

The ending of seeking brings on a new dimension of fun. This communication is like playing soccer. Passing the ball is happening. Penalty's are happening. Goals are happening. Nobody is kicking the ball. It's all fun!

GOOD ON YA, No One!

And there (here) "IT" IS, glaringly obvious never lost never found. Being-Awareness-Aliveness. Welcome Back to The Home You Never Left.

61. Form Is Emptiness Is Form. Not Two ...

Final Follow-up from A.J. - *Thank you Charlie for the powerful answer to my question! As long as there's been Life here I've never (on investigation) discovered any 'me' or substantial 'entity' at the steering wheel.*

There is truly no-one here. That has always and ever been the case. From early childhood on this one burning question has been on my mind: 'What the xxx is going on???'

Eventually I learned that NOTHING IS GOING ON OR HAPPENING. There is just BOUNDLESS-INFINITE-SPACE-LIKE-MYSTERY wherein a lot appears to happen. A life story is apparently happening including everything that goes with it. The elusiveness of it all is utterly obvious.

My true condition is a non-position. As our common friend Tony Parsons puts it, I AM "Nothing being everything". The Buddha says in the heart-sutra: 'Emptiness is Form, Form is Emptiness'. Those words are the core of Buddhism. It is the description of Dharmakaya. It is: THIS IS IT !

It is the ineffable put into sound.

LOVE BOUNDLESS !!!!

YUP. And THAT is THAT. You. Or ... Love.

Love Says ...... Hello, Love! Welcome Home.

62. Who gets "Irritated" by a Teaching?

About a particular non-duality teaching, M.K. Writes: ... *there is something about the presentation that periodically causes irritation. Like when he talks about Ramana being dualistic and then himself slips into dualistic descriptions once in a while.*

Sure. That's the paradoxical nature of using words to point Beyond to the Infinite Isness. Isn't it interesting that "some thing" gets "irritated?" What gets irritated?? Only a self-center (the false sense of being apart from the whole) can be kind of annoyed or offended. So that happens. My sense of that teacher is that he likes to say outrageous stuff, to "stir the pot" that way, and then perhaps the seeker-mind reacts, then there may be a noticing of a false "irritated me." It's a style of expression, but there is no-one "doing" that! It's appearing to happen ... as mind IS all the appearing happenings ... the Dream-World of seeker/teacher.

Do you agree with him when he says that doing inquiry is totally useless and impossible?

No. But NOR do "I" "disagree"! This pointing happens in a million ways. The pointer points and the mind agrees or disagrees ... ONLY the mind does that. THAT is where an an expression such as that can prick something and begin to let some of the false concepts be seen into ... that is just another "take" on all this ... nobody is doing anything.

It is also the nature of mind to take a few words out of context and then analyze them apart from the entirety of a message ... For accuracy the pointer coming through all these "organism-speakings" is NOT that it is useless and impossible to inquire into the false and thereby dispel it. That one is always saying there IS no one to do or not do anything.

All is just appearing as happenings ... including "doing inquiry." In other places he says exactly that.

I do not want to throw out the baby with the water though.

Okay, now WHO is wanting to do THAT or not do that? Stay with the simplicity:

A) What you are is Awareness-Noticing ... the silent Seeing it-self of all that is appearing on the screen of that Awareness. NOT the se-er and NOT the seen: The See-ING.

B) What you are NOT is any thing that "you" can "know. Stay with the Final Question: WHO AM I?

WHO cares what "another" says? WHO cares about opinions of agree and disagree, right and wrong, this and that? WHO??

63. There's No 'me' BUT ...

A. Writes (on YouTube) ... *I am thoroughly enjoying your videos and love the excitement that arises when I see you've uploaded a new one. I am also so grateful for the new Jeff Foster videos. His book "Life without a Centre" dispersed some clouds for me.*

Jeff is a good expresser of the inexpressible! But watch how the mind-ego grabs the dispersal of clouds of confusion and says, "clouds dispersed – for ME."

Like most of the folks who write to you, I intellectually understand what is being said.

Drop the label "intellectually. What's left? "I understand." Now drop the "I" from that. What's left? "Understand-ING"... with no "understand-ER." In this way it is seen that This Presence-Awareness has ALWAYS been the NON-Conceptual Impersonal Understand-ing -- Just THAT – that in which "I" and "Intellectual" arise as thoughts ... labeling this What Is-Ness and seeming to create a separateness where none actually exists. The word "intellectual" was learned; the one-letter word "I" was learned. Before that happened there was only This Presence. For my 20-month-old granddaughter Sarah there is NO "I." That has not been taken on board yet; she is just Aliveness Dancing! This is why it is said often, all knowledge (beginning with the learned-knowledge of "I and Other") is actually IGNORANCE!

This "triad" of "knower-I" and "knowing-of" and "object-known" is false; on direct seeing where IS this "I"? Is there any such thing? "Know-ING" or "Understand-ING" IS. THAT never changes ever!

So: YOU were NEVER a subject observing objects – that's the appearance of dualism, separateness. You are untouchable ever-fresh Being-Awareness, Aliveness, Just That. What Jeff calls "Life without a Centre" is pointing to THIS .... Aliveness, or Life Itself, devoid of the false belief in a subject-object reality. What is real? Unchanging presence-awareness. Only That.

I've also had a lengthy blissful experience that is sticking like some residue in the mind.

Oh yes. Been there got the t-shirt! THAT is one of the worst things that can happen to the seeker because it sets up a big fat MYTH: That was IT and "I" was "DONE! Now "IT" is GONE O Poor Me I "MUST Get That Back ad nauseaum! The parable in the Christian Bible of "The Wedding Feast" comes to mind: Entering the Wedding Feast with the wrong attire, the guest is thrown out into the dark cold night and there is "much weeping and wailing and gnashing of teeth." That's a metaphor, it seems here, for this "entering the kingdom of heaven with the wrong attire:" The persona, the mask of an "I" identity, a "ME" that is HERE in the Kingdom O Praise God Thank God O God DOES love ME because "He" (Or SHE!) let "ME" into HIS/HER Special Heavenly STATE! It's bullshit and that "me" soon gets its comeuppance and then there is the seeking back tenfold! Isn't that your experience?

So, "IT" did not "go away." You came back and claimed your own absence, and that happens a LOT. It happened here in 2002, again in 2004, again in 2005.

You'd think it would be seen through if it happened once, but some patterns of energy SEEM more solid and stubbornly steadfast in declaring "I'm ME and that's that!" over and over ... that's what seems to happen. Of course none of that is actually happening – it's the DREAM!

There's always the dull drone of "get that back. I must get that back, if it doesn't feel like that it ain't it" and then the thought "no you mustn't wish for an experience, stop it!" I'm having a hard time seeing the second as just a thought arising.

Who is having a "hard time?" Who "must or must not" anything? Ask that apparent person, that I – I – I - I you go on about, WHO ARE YOU? Ask yourself, WHO AM I? This is NOT a feeling, NOT an experience. Those are appearances, like clouds in an always-actually-empty sky, that come and go. All that appears comes and goes in This Being, the Unchanging Space-like Awareness that you actually are.

Annette Nibley's writings are laser sharp and I enjoy them, yet as I read, the thought arises "Why are you reading this if you've got it already!" and there is a subtle discomfort, a feeling of betrayal.

Betrayal? To whom? Annette? There IS NO Annette! She'll be the first to tell ya that! Or betrayal to YOU? Your True Self? How can THAT be? You must be separating yourself in thoughts being believed to be about you, and true, for such stories to be taken seriously. "I'm ME." IS THAT TRUE? Have a look.

There's no me here, but I feel it with every fiber of my being.

You contradict yourself with every concept. That's what the mind does. "There's no me BUT I Feel It." What a load of crap THAT is! However, this is how it seems for many seekers, NOT as an apparent thought of "me," but as a kind of sense-feeling or "feeling-sense," deep down. This feeling-sense IS only a believed-in-thought, this "I" we discussed above – BUT it does SEEM that this is not a thought but something "I" feel – as you say, "*feeling with every fiber of my being.*"

But notice the words! “MY BEING.” WHOSE being is it? Yours? WHO claims to be “me” apart from BEING? WHO IS THAT! Look. Ask! Who AM I? Who do I take myself to be? A seeker still incomplete and searching for peace?

Is that just "me" arising right now? And it feels so real? It's an uncomfortable feeling, knowing there isn't a me yet feeling like there is one. A phantom "me", so to speak.

Asked and answered.

When I recite "I am" I tend to believe more in the "me". When I ask the question who's the doer, I answer: "I am," and it feels plausible.

It's not about “reciting,” it's about looking. And the answer is NOT what we are looking for. ALL conceptual knowing, EVEN the conceptual knowledge “I am,” IS Ignorance. ASK and take NO answer. Not That Not That. Drop all answers as they arise and just ASK. Paraphrasing Nisargadatta, drop ALL answers and questions except this one thought: Who Am I?

That “I AM” you BELIEVE is “YOU” is ONLY a thought. It’s the mind’s translation of the pure NON-conceptual Isness of Being One-Without-A-Second, Being-Awareness, into the “thought-form of I.” And a thought “I”, or “I AM,” is NOT a separate, actual independent thing; it is an ephemeral, temporary appearance that comes and goes in Unchanging Presence-Awareness. So, be willing to DROP all answers and abide as NOT Knowing. Unknowing Presence-Awareness; Cluelessly Being This, as it is and as it ain’t. FULL STOP.

Seeking an answer IS the denial of this Presence, Being-Aliveness ... you attempt to find Being, and that’s like a fish in the ocean seeking the water: “Where O Where is my Water?

I MUST find THAT or I shall Suffer Forever!" It is the "tale told by an idiot, filled with sound and fury, signifying – NOTHING."

I'm looking for bliss, aren't I?

Yes, and you'll NEVER get there! YOU ARE "BLISS" (that's just a fancy word for ever-fresh never-absent Timeless Being.) Seeking that IS the DENIAL of THAT.

When I imagine seeking a remedy, I realize the futility of it, yet I feel hopeless.

BE with that. Now ask, WHO feels?

I know there is no one here...

Let's get real and play Hardball! LOOK: That's your bullshit. If you truly know there is no one, all that you are saying would never be said ... by you! The "Fabulous Enlightened Ego" says, "I know there is no one here. That is a flat LIE. <u>Stop</u> with this "knowing" already!

... yet, I feel the body sensations of anxiety and fear. I still care what others think of me or fear harm from others. I still try and calculate the best outcome for my future... I still cringe over a past indiscretion. I'm stuck believing this will all go away and I can't understand why it wouldn't. I'm really trapped in the mind and can't seem to escape.

I I I! WHO?? Don't be lazy to look, to ask, to find out what you are NOT.

And there's the question "Who would escape?" and I'd answer "me the one who's trapped. "Who's trapped?" Ah, how is it that

I'm seen trapped in the mind? The me and the mind has been noted, yet not by the me nor the mind...

Essentially, I still feel I have to DO SOMETHING other than just witness...

So long as you believe there is a “me” there that IS a doer and therefore suffer, DO the one Final Question and accept NO answer. Keep asking, WHO AM I? After all you are directly inescapably BEING. What or WHO you are NOT is not yet seen: When the final question is exhausted, there you are as always, standing alone, free and clear, Being that Presence-Awareness Alive as Life Itself. This is the Eternal Home You never Left … Unchanging Being. Only That and NOTHING else.

The thought "I am" is a self-reinforcing thought of a mistaken identity! We prove we are separate by proving it with thought. This is seen through when there is an earnestness to investigate: "I Am. Is That True? Can I know absolutely that I am the thought 'I am'?" No. The proof that this thought "I am" is not the True I AM of NON-conceptual Being Its Self is available by seeing right now that in deep sleep there IS no thought of "I am," and yet Life lives the body organism. If YOU are the "thought I am" than YOU would die when sleep happens, and YOU do NOT. I AM IS. That is NOT a thought. NOT a feeling. It just .... IS! See that right now and that's the end of the search.

Note: Remember this from Wei Wu Wei?“*Even the intellectual understanding of the inexistence of our 'selves' is a rare and bitter attainment which few even attempt. And that is only the elimination round which qualifies us for access to Reality... Intellectual understanding should be not indispensable to a 'simple' mind, but, with our conditioning, it would seem to be an almost inevitable preliminary.*”

"The mind produces thoughts ceaselessly, even when you do not look at them. When you know what is going on in your mind, you call it consciousness. This is your waking state - your consciousness shifts from sensation to sensation, from perception to perception, from idea to idea, in endless succession. Then comes awareness, the direct insight into the whole of consciousness, the totality of the mind. The mind is like a river, flowing ceaselessly in the bed of the body; you identify yourself for a moment with some particular ripple and call it "my thought". All you are conscious of is your mind; awareness is the cognizance of consciousness as a whole."

-Sri Nisargadatta Maharaj

64. There Is No Such Thing As A Sage

E.P Writes, *Can the sage feel deep depression? I can see there's no me, but feelings arise...*

First off, are you assuming there is such a "thing" as a "sage?"

Let's look: What is a sage?

A four-letter word. That word is a movement of sound in the space of Aware Presence … that which you know to be always here before, during and after thoughts, words, feelings, all that "arises" as you put it.

Depression is, bluntly, FALSE. All suffering is conceptual and therefore impermanent. Nothing that comes and goes can fit the simple test for Eternal Reality: That which is the Unchanging Knowing Presence, the open emptiness that all that arises, arises within. Overlooking this ever-present awareness of being, simply ordinary empty awareness that is PRIOR to all thoughts and stories, IS the ignorance of the dividing mind-stuff.

What some call "the sage" is nothing whatsoever that can be known or experienced. The word, like all words, is pointing to this Awareness that knows no division within Itself. That is all. Allow that forgetting of the Presence to subside, as it does between, before and after every thought and feeling, no matter how "fierce" or "benign."

The pointer is, what you are is that Aware Presence of Being Itself; everything that arises and subsides appears IN that … like the thunderclouds or tornadoes or wisps of cumulus appear and disappear along with apparent (conceptual) “time” in that vast, unbounded space of the sky itself.

Let go of trying to understand, know that concepts are not real and only that Unchanging Beingness is true and real … and let this Awareness show you it’s Loving Accepting Presence.

65. Pain Is Distinct From Suffering

Follow-up from E.P. - *The thing is, I guess I am mistaking pain with suffering. They seem to be all together. It's too deeply rooted, and I guess my mistake is to see that every time I have negative emotions (sadness, worry, anxiety etc.) it feels as I am doing something wrong regarding spirituality. That it just shouldn't be this way... :(*

There is suffering in ALL ideas of I should (or should NOT) about anything that is happening in Being-Awareness.

But I still have the feeling that the pain, even knowing that there is no separate 'me' to feel it, is no good and has to go away....if you can say anything else regarding your personal experience in this subject, I would be pleased!

Let's keep it very simple and clear: When there is arthritis or back pain here, I take painkillers!

What is INCLUDED in all that is, IS the ideation that "I don't like this and need to correct it." No problem. THAT is the perfectly functioning organism-identity that knows there is pain and needs to do something about it. That is all perfectly practical and the “sage” has all these things happening. Life is no different for the “sage” in these ways. What IS different is the absence of the added idea of, as you say, “I am doing something wrong regarding spirituality. That it just shouldn't be this way.”

WHO is telling WHOM? Who is believing this load of lies? I am not attacking YOU, only that ideation which makes you suffer. Consider this: You listen to thoughts with a conviction they refer to YOU. That is a sign of deep ignorance: The stubborn ego IGNORES the Truth of Being-Awareness and believes its own lies about what is real, what is spiritual, what ought to be happening or not happening etc. ad nauseum!

That is a dreamed character named E.P. trying to alter, modify or correct the dream.

See that this false identification with an idea of being someone who "should be some other way" IS the core of suffering. I would like to see you doing a much deeper inquiry into what is actually happening and into this idea that YOU are suffering the pains of all that emotional stuff. Meanwhile, it may be appropriate for you to get medical help. For many years I was on Prozac, to address a chemical imbalance. It worked brilliantly.

If something is broke you want to fix it. There is nothing "unspiritual" about that! What gets added on to the simple pain and desire to repair what's not working is ideas like "this not liking pain means I ... I! .. am not a very spiritual; person." WHO or WHAT is this "I?"

There is often the totally FALSE idea that enlightenment or realization "means" that there is only bliss and joy and that when there is no peace of mind or when there are preferences that arise that "means," "I am not enlightened." The realization of the absence of any separate egoic entity that has happened through the sage is NOT "peace of mind!" There is never any possibility for permanent peace of mind: the so-called mind is nothing but a thought, the "I" thought, which has been mistakenly believed to be who you are, and then added on to and appended over years and years until the habit is so strong that who you are has seemed to disappear and all that is left is a suffering thought-person. But that is all a dream!!!!

There is NO such thing as eternal peace of mind.

The peace of the so-called Sage (and there is NO such thing as a "sage!") is BEYOND the machinations of the dual mind; it is that Silence which is what you truly are; that Silent "substrate" or backdrop, which is like a vast multi-dimensional cinema screen on which this dream-movie show appears, and two of the characters appearing on the screen appear to be typing, reading and thinking ... the characters called E.P. and Charlie. That backdrop of Aware Silence IS "The Peace that passeth understanding." It is never missing, and never was. It is simply being overlooked!

All that is happening when there is suffering is the mistake of identification and it only stands due to lack of investigation!

Look. Look deeply with a commitment to get down to it. What worked for me is to keep looking, and to NOT accept any answer to the questions, "Who am I?" What is my real nature? What is real and what is NOT real?" (Ultimately it may dawn on "you" that "you" are not real and therefor that "you" has NO such thing as a "true nature").

In any case it appears that this must happen. I sincerely hope it happens for you. Realize though that what is being pointed to is not so much a prescription for a doing as a description of the earnestness to end suffering that arises in an organism (your own organism, right there right now) from what we might call Grace. Or, just good fortune.

YOU are That Which Never Changes. Nothing that changes is actually real. But YOU need to look earnestly and deeply -- and give up that you know anything at all. Especially with regard to "enlightenment" or "self-realization." Dwell in the Unknowing I AM Awareness. This is NOT a thought process! The answer is NOT in the mind or language! Keep going deeper!

66. Who Is Worried?

Follow-up from E.P. - *I will ask you some time to digest this email on pain and suffering, which is very important to me, but I would like already to ask you something: You said somewhere,*

"The realization of the absence of any separate egoic entity that has happened through "the sage" is NOT "peace of mind!" There is never any possibility for permanent peace of mind: the so-called mind is nothing but a thought, the "I" thought, which has been mistakenly believed to be who you are, and then added on to and appended over years and years until the habit is so strong that who you are has seemed to disappear and all that is left is a suffering person. But that is all a dream!!!!"

As an exercise, as I've been understanding very well what is Truth, and what is Dream (thoughts like these), I just tried to talk with a friend today to get some other point of view, and kept myself put in Being. No problem. Everything ok. But I ask you: I guess I still have the feeling that on the realized sage he just wouldn't have this momentary thought disorder (right after a situation in which I felt disinterest in a loved one, I felt a deep discomfort, which extended until today...now my energy is stabilizing). I mean, it could even last for longer.

Anything can appear in this "dream of 'me'." It ALL comes and goes. What never comes and goes? Look into that.

This discomfort in the body appeared after these thoughts, but I guess I still think that on the sage it would be just different.

Who said so? You listen to the mind feed you these myths and stories and think they are real, only because you ignore the Is-ness of it and focus on the "shouldness" of the ignorant mind!

As I told you before, I still have this deeply rooted PREJUDICE against the EMOTIONAL PAINS CREATED BY THOUGHTS as something that WOULD BE BETTER CONTROLLED ON A SAGE. Is this so? If so, how can I manage it better?

I really urge a deeper look: WHO is worried and WHO is the "I" that "must be losing interest?" All that is a conversation, an OVERLAY that is distinct from what actually happens.

Rather than ask other's experience, bring it home to your OWN experience. This suffering is optional. But hearing that makes no real difference unless you LOOK for yourself.

PS: Things are really getting clearer and clearer, as a result of my earnestness for all these years of search (since 2002). Advaita is getting really into the point, very sharply. Thank you!

You are most welcome.

67. Who Endlessly Asks WHY?

Follow-up from E.P. - *I was wondering.....why spiritual traditions give some much emphasis on quietening the thoughts and emotions, IF WE ARE NOT THE THOUGHTS NOR THE EMOTIONS. I've been realizing it just doesn't need to be quiet. It's irrelevant!*

Have "you" slipped back into believing you are a person who wants answers and asks why why why??

Who's asking the question? Is there is a dreamed character, "E.P.," who asks another dreamed character about the dream, all the while believing the dream to be the real?

All this arises in What Never Changes. What is it that NEVER CHANGES? Ask YOU. Who are you? ASK! Who AM I? WHO wants to know? WHO!!??

Thoughts and emotions are simply movements of energy, Awareness Presence arising as what appears and disappears. All this arises in What Never Changes. What is it that NEVER CHANGES?

All those ignorant teachings fall short. A quiet mind is still a mind .. an idea of a person, a “me” ... and what you are is OUTSIDE the so-called mind and all its machinations!

What Never Changes!!??

Presence, Being, the pure Space-Like I AM-ness .. can and does appear as ALL that is. No separation exists anywhere and even the thought of separation, of two-ness, IS what IS and NOT actually apart from That. Being is all there is. Nothing appearing as everything. Full Stop.

Forget spiritual traditions. They are dead words appearing to a dream character who still wants to know "why." WHO is asking the questions? WHO wants to know? WHO!?

Drop it and BE.

68. Freedom Is Being Naked Awareness

E.P. writes another follow-up: *I was wondering....the beauty of Truth is that ANYBODY, in any external condition (miserable, sick, wealthy etc.) has the same opportunity to recognize himself as peace, since it's present in any living being. It's just a matter of recognition.*

In a way, yes. However, the story of "persons" in various "conditions" is ONLY a story. There are no persons in Naked Awareness as-It-is.

This sets me free from HAVING to struggle in order to maintain these external condition up.

You are getting to the heart of this now. There is NO suffering or struggle in what you TRULY are... Aware Presence, or Presence-Awareness. Livingness goes on effortlessly in this Space-Like Unbounded Presence, the Impersonal Being-Nature.

But when you assert "this sets ME free" there is still a little mental confusion arising. WHO is this "me" that has "been set free?"

This Naked Freedom is NOT personal. That does not "set any 'me' free." The "me" is ONLY a false idea of a "real separate person" who "was bound and is now free." There IS no such thing, as the self-investigation reveals. (As you know the "investigation" is carried out through questioning every thought and feeling... "Who thinks? Who feels?" And so on: Ultimately, "Who am I?" .... Accepting NO answer.)

So using language (inherently limited) as best we can to point, let us drop "I am free" in favor of "there is Freedom."

That gets closer to the Reality of This, but of course these words are still ONLY a concept, a pointer. Don't start worshiping pointers; they are NOT the "truth."

Don't believe a word of any of this!

In any event, You (the Real You, The "Naked I", which the mind translates, using language, to "I Am,") are already always freedom itself, and were never bound; the cage of thoughts was never actually real. Freedom is an impersonal recognition of that and NOT a "personal attainment." When some person announces, "I am free," I cringe, because its clear in the space of freedom itself that there is no such thing as a "free person!" That's the final trap; it does seem that many go through this particular stage (including this writer, "to whom" it did seem to happen, in this dream.)

Remember: "Find what is it that never sleeps and never wakes, and whose pale reflection is our sense of 'I'." (Sri Nisargadatta).

Just see this from nowhere ... right now: Knowing ... that IMPERSONAL knowing-ness ... that what You are, the Real Infinite I-Ness, IS that Naked Awareness in which "you" appear ... THIS is a blow to the false from "The Naked I" of freedom-presence itself. But THAT I ("I - I" distinct from "I am me") is NON-conceptual.

If there is still a subtle as yet un-fully-examined belief in two-ness (as in "I know who I am") that can (and nearly always will) claim the knowing as "my" knowing, just see that this is a subtle resistance of the ego-idea to its own demise. To paraphrase the poet "Ram Tzu," you seek personal ascendance where there is (in Reality) only Impersonal Transcendence.

So: Don't let the ego CLAIM that as "ITS" attainment, my friend. THIS ... Seeing with Naked Awareness ... is, as we always point out over and over, NOT "personal." Just see that claiming mechanism operating through Naked Awareness, and this ... Seeing ... is enough to toast the false and then (now) only the Real is left, so to speak. But THAT, Real Awareness, was ACTUALLY never missing. What a joke – and the joke's on "me."

All right? So, in summary, THIS SEEING is the clear Presence of Awareness ... and the ABSENCE of the person who "is aware." Just a little caution here to not let the ego claim any big enlightenment; that can bring suffering again in a flash. Stay vigilant. And remember, the idea of a person, even a person called "anybody," is false. There is NO person anywhere, not in you nor anywhere else. The person is a dream, a phantom. Seeing with Naked Awareness IS the RE-Cognition. THAT Essence is RE Cognized, but only now. Right now you are That. Period, Full Stop. You are seeing this. All conditions evaporate in That Seeing and there is nothing left to resist, attain, avoid or seek. That Naked Awareness IS the Home you never left.

I mean, knowing who I am, means I have all I need for the moment. In any condition!!! That's a beautiful realization!

Now you know. So stay put, and don't let the mind-ego story convince you that its lies are true ever again.

By the way, you have been a great help for me...thank you really!!

You are very welcome, E.P. Your own openness is a great gift ... you might call that gift "Grace."

69. Who Cares?

E.P. Writes once again, *Yes, and you know what? I don't care anymore if questions arise. That's all mind stuff and it doesn't define anything. As I told you, I've been for so long trying to be still, quiet-mind, no worry, no anger, being in good health, as the 'gurus' advised me to, but it's all irrelevant.*

So, no more anxieties, no more suffering? Good on ya. Being ... Only That. Enjoy the Now...

As a matter of fact, poor health could be still fixed. To live from our noumenon essence doesn't imply having do let go of the phenomenon. Like, I've been for a while having trouble to sleep, and the organism feels horrible during the day...maybe it's a matter on strengthening the sleeping pills. It's amazing how our society and yoga invests so much in the perfection of the personality, maybe because they still take peace as an attained perfection of the organism. Peace lies in the noumenon. Awareness recognizing itself.

Exactly. Well said.

70. WHO Suffers?

E.P. Follows up again, *The intelligence energy moves our actions, and all the trouble is caused by the egoic overlays...like by thinking:" I should be more hardworking than I am"*

Yep. That's the suffering. But for who!??

Sailor Bob says we should stay put in Being, and never mind to the egoic thinking... Should we just manifest our innate self instead of following the ego's suggestions, or mind could be of a great help sometimes?

WHO asks this question?? Give up all questions but this one: WHO AM I? As we say here over and over!

Maybe the only problem is the suffering caused by intense egoic overlay, which has nothing to do with planning or trying to improve our external conditions.... But it is hard to figure out when mind 'claims mastery' and when it is just a good servant...using it as a tool it is just fine, but sometimes it gets too annoying!!

Drop this by asking WHO is telling this story? WHO?

DO this! ASK WHO AM I? As long as you believe you are the one telling the story you make the story more real than Presence-Awareness. ASK YOU, WHO AM I? Take NO answer. Follow the sage Ramana Maharshi's pointer:

"The thought 'Who am I?' will destroy all other thoughts, and like the stick used for stirring the burning pyre, it will itself in the end get destroyed. Then, there will arise Self-Realization."

There is a lovely paradox in all this: While there is in Truth no such thing as a separate "I" and you already ARE what you seek, as long as there is the false BELIEF in a "me, myself, I" then this investigation is clearly called for.

It's now time for the Ruthless Truthless Truth.

LOOK: There is no sage. That's a thought - story. It's a manner of speaking about That which is IMPERSONAL. That's all; there is no enlightened person, no enlightened organism. There are no "enlightened sages"!

YOU are NOT a story. NOR will "you" ever "attain sagehood!" It is all nonsense. Just STOP believing these LIES. Right Now.

If you REALLY see there is no "me" then who is asking these questions? Your claim of seeing is, to be blunt, crap! In seeing there is no "me" there is no one left to claim a that seeing! There is no "you" to "see" that.

It's this simple... "you"do not exist.

LOOK! All there is is Awareness, Presencing. Oneness, Onenessing. There is no "depression" or "suffering" in Awareness. THAT is a product of your still believing you are a separate entity. This is the last time I will say this to you: LOOK for that "person" and you find ... Nothing.

Go and do the LOOKING. BAKE in the oven of these pointers.

You are that Nothing. Full Stop!

There is no separate "you." But until that's clear keep at it.

KEEP LOOKING for the "one who owns depression." There is NO suffering in Awareness; ONLY in the mind, the me story. You are pretending to be a "POOR ME!"

What never changes? Take your stand in That.

Now stop and BAKE in the pointers. No more questions for now, okay? GO BAKE!

71. No Answer – That is IT

Yet another follow-up from E.P. - *I never went too much into this self-inquiry because I never had a "correct" answer to it.*

But now, I'm seeing that is not answerable, it is just a direct 'coming back' experience of our nature....yesterday and to-day I have been asking and asking, and it comes back to a void...

It's been really powerful...

Excellent.

Just being what this organism is up to be... Hurt feelings, joyfulness, a mix of emotions, ups and downs, but....WHO SAID IT SHOULDN'T BE?? AS IT IS IS AS IT IS! No egoic involvement, or maybe yes sometimes, even that is out of my control.....:) What's left?

Not Nothing. Not Everything.
Not emptiness not Fullness.
Neither nonexistent nor eternal
Not subject nor object
Neither Immaculate Nor Vulgar
There It Is NOT. There It IS!

Not One. Not Two.
Neither absent nor present,
Not absence not presence
Not ignorance not wisdom
Neither here nor there,
No mind no being.
Naked Awareness. Just This. Nothing Else.

72. Late To The Party

Have you noticed that thoughts arrive in the brain as a commentary after the fact of whatever is appearing?

There is a split second delay between the moment of a thought forming and the recognition of that thought as it appears in the brain. It goes like this: The bodymind stands up. Then the thought "I stood up" happens ... after the fact.

73. Everything Reveals This Peace

A few weeks pass, then arrives a wonderful follow-up from E.P:

I've been maturing and realizing who the heck I am after all, and it has been very comforting. The sense of separation has dropped away, on by seeing clearly the essence of Being in everything and as everything. Even body anxiety is dropping... Sometimes there is just the relaxation to the moment, and even on listening to the cars on the street is a revelation of this peace that is everywhere...as it is! I just wanted to share that with you.

That's GREAT news, E.P.

All gets naturally resolved in the Unborn. Love Ya!

74. A Spiritual Movie Show Passing Here

R.G. Writes, *"I" feel that almost every time the thought of "I" or "me" slides by the mind its often exposed by awareness. and lately, in the persistence of this sort of "watching" (it seems like "I'm" persisting, but I know its not so) ...*

All that you are describing the passing show. A particularly “spiritual” movie, it seems! But what IS the I – I – I?

All this is happening in what you are ... ordinary blank slate awareness-presence. This that you are is untouched by the fantasy-show passing along an imaginary time line. There is nothing wrong or right with any of this. It simply IS … like clouds, some wispy, some dark and stormy, in the empty sky. This Aware Presence that you are is not a watcher or a witness, nor an experience of void or emptiness. It (YOU) IS. That is all. IT IS. And that is two words too many.

Space-like Awareness is NOT an object “known” by the false subject (mind.)

When you say “I know it is not so,” there is the ego-mind CLAIMING the Understanding for itself; it is subtle, it claims its own absence! That is something that seems to occur often as the Absolute Nondual Understanding takes hold. This Nondual Seeing or Understanding is like a “Good” Cancer that eats away at all the false egoic beliefs in volition and free will. Then it tries to keep a sense of control by claiming it “gets it.” That could be called “spiritual ego.”

It happens along the way. But all of this is simply a happening, and what you are stands in the clear, unseen and unknowable in the way the imaginary ego-mind takes concepts on board, because it wants to “know it knows”!

It is insecure and so it wants to know that it comprehends, and grasps this and owns it. So it will feel safe.

But it's ALL imagination! You will never get this in the mind. The mind is only a thought, the "I" thought, and as such, mind is an object that appears and goes away. Can a thought see or do anything?

What is that which Never Changes? The "I" comes and goes, as you report in this email. Look right now: what Never Changes? In waking, dreaming, deep sleep? That Thou Art.

There are experiences in the mind and body of a kind of automatic nature.. almost as if mind, body, world, universe, even awakeness itself, is sort of self contained. like no ones running the show. of course I've read this many times, but never experienced it first hand!

Treat this experience as just another "spiritual experience." A momentary happening. Then the mind wants to turn that into a "truth" that it "knows." That is all that is happening. My good friend John Greven described a similar happening (I recommend you get his very good book "Oneness") and he shared how it was finally seen that this seeing, while it may be "the way it is," it is still appearing and disappearing in the timeless spaceless Being ... Eternal, Natural, Absolute Freedom.

Anything that comes and goes cannot be the Eternal State. Eternity is not "a real long time."

What is this knowing presence of awareness, or awareness of presence, BEFORE the mind? That which is never "off," never missing, ever-fresh, ever-present? See that all the stories and experiences are about dead imaginary pasts and all fears of "what about me, what is happening to me" are dead imaginary futures.

As John Wheeler pointed out to me, Presence is never more or less present. Awareness is never more or less aware! Who is it that believes there is a solid separate 'me" that can be threatened?? Who is it that is convinced that there is such a "thing" as "time?" This endless beginningless Now Awareness is absolute and untouched by all that arises in it. Who thinks? Who types and reads and feels? WHO?

Also i know that experience can only ever be experience and that's where it ends, but when this is revealed, it feels like "me" but not "me" because this (we'll say big me nobody) is looking at this automatic existence and even the very awakeness itself!

There is no "big me." That is the false claiming mechanism of the imaginary ego wanting to maintain its identity. All just another appearance in what You are – Presence Awareness, emptiness. But look for this "me" ... 'big me" or "little me" ... and you will not find anything ... this is the investigation needed: Seek the source of the "I Am" idea, find out if there really IS any such entity as a separate "me" (even the really huge "me" that is space-like and all encompassing. What is being pointed to is NOT an object that mind can grasp and own. "I am Nothing, or I am God" seems in some cases to be a last stand of the false idea of separation. That is an idea of an personal entity claiming to be an impersonal being. Who is this one? What is the source of all this? Is there a source? Is separation real? For whom?

The question "Who Am I" can unravel all this IF you steadfastly refuse ANY answer. Just ask the question: Who Am I? Who Am I? Again: Here's what the great Sage Sri Ramana Maharshi said on this "method" of investigation into the false: "The thought 'Who am I?' will destroy all other thoughts, and like the stick used for stirring the burning pyre, it will itself in the end get destroyed. Then, there will arise Self-Realization."

And also again: There is a lovely paradox in all this: While there is in Truth no such thing as a separate "I' and you already ARE what you seek, as long as there is the false BELIEF in a "me, myself, I" then this investigation is clearly called for.

I know none of this can be understood by the mind, because "it" (awareness) sees the mind, body, world, senses.

Who is claiming to "know" this?!? Awareness does not see! There is seeing happening in Awareness. The false ego-mind in its ignorance claims Awareness as a thing that sees! Awareness is NOT a perceiving object. Awareness is nothing! No Thing. NOT an object. Awareness IS all that is. IT is all there is. Awareness, Consciousness is all there is. All there is is Awareness, Consciousness. Being-Awareness-Loving to be. That is what you really are. Not Two. Not Two. Not Two.

But there is a definite change in the way existence is experienced! or so it seems...

Okay, WHO "knows" this? Who experiences this ... or not? What is that on which change happens?? (Like the movie appears on the blank screen.) Investigate these claims of the false ego-mind: Who Am I? ASK ASK ASK. Who Am I? Accept No answer!! Who Am I? Not That. Who Am I? Not That. Ask until the questioner dissolves and there will be what was never missing and is there (here) right now: Self-shining Presence, the Light of UN-Knowing Awareness. Just That and nothing else!

I've also watched your video about anxiety. [Note the conversations with E.P. earlier in this book, that was the stimulus for the video] *That explained a lot. I've experienced anxiety much throughout this awakening, mostly due to the mind sporadically realizing that it's not in control of anything!! Even movement of limbs!*

It's damn hard to "let" anxiety or downright panic happen. even though it just does. is this crazy?? It feels, at times, like mind is dying or something, and its fighting with fear and panic. Especially at Walmart! (no joke).

Oaky ... but, all that is also an appearance in the endless open sky of Empty Being. What is crazy is accepting the false (the idea of being a separate entity) as real. This is simply a crazy mistake that started around the age of two or three when the belief formed that there is "me" and "other than me."

Fear is the idea that there is an entity to be threatened by scary "others" (people at Walmart? I don't find any such 'others' in the Walmart here!)

Investigate the false and it will be seen (by no one) that all there is, is Awareness-Presence, appearing as all this play of consciousness. You are not a concept or object that can be hurt... or touched in any way. Get down to this investigation straight away. Are you the body? Are you the thinker? Who says so? Who? Stop accepting hearsay. Find your own Truth right here right now. And do stay in touch. Let's get this ended for you right now.

Anyway, I guess my question is: Is this normal or am I crazy?

YES.

75. Some Good Investigation and It Is Done

Follow-up from R.G. - *Thank you!! after reading this about 20 times, writing, asking more questions, seems un- needed so to speak. the question "who am i" ... answer " i am me?" question: " who is me?" " i don't know!" "who doesn't know??? who's asking " who doesn't know?!!" and on and on. the question " who am i" even seems ridiculous " to whom does it seem..?" ha!!*

Bingo! And that was pretty fast ... happy to hear it has dawned on no-one that there is only Nothing/Everything!

So there you have it! A little deep investigation and seeking ends, usually with a hearty laugh!

76. Much Ado About Nothing

A note arrives from J.H., a visitor to a "Gift Of Unknowing" Meeting: *I want to say...Thanks. You are a terrific and loving presence. I will never forget your kindness, openness and your relentless pointing. Much Ado About Nothing indeed :-)*

It takes One to "know" One :-)

77. Is This All There Is?

A Friend writes: (Remember the song?)

Is that all there is, is that all there is
If that's all there is my friends, then let's keep dancing
Let's break out the booze and have a ball
If that's all there is

That really sad song by Peggy Lee could be America's anthem. We can almost hear that refrain humming ever so faintly in the background as we try to fill the bottomless void that we refer to as 'me'.

Ahhhh. What if THIS is as good as it gets?!? LOL.

Reminds me of an old New Yorker cartoon by Gahan Wilson: Two monks sitting in Zazen meditation. One old, wizened, stunningly existentially resigned -- like Sartre when he wrote "No Exit" or "The Nausea." One young monk, wearing a questioning look. The caption is, "Nothing happens next. This is it."

This existential despair in that Peggy Lee song bespeaks the "half baked" approach to Nonduality, where emptiness is taken on board as "my" emptiness. Despair inevitably ensues! So long as there is a person, a false entity, at play, then that entity when faced with its own inauthenticity, will nearly always rail in defense, moaning about the "emptiness and meaningless" of "my" life and life itself. This apparent emptiness of "me" is a disaster of epic proportions to the ego ... being confronted by it's own unreality, it struggles to maintain "order" and "volition." Hello ... been there done that got the bloody "Prozac" T-shirt. There were years ... decades! ... of deep depression when this idea of "me being nothing" was believed. That pointer that "this is it" and "life is empty and meaningless" ... only a conceptual

POINTER and not "the truth" ... was taken on board as a description of "my life." That is adding meaning where there is none: That is often the ego-mind mechanism's last line of defense as its citadel of concepts is being stormed by Naked Truth! Hey: It is empty and meaningless that its empty and meaningless, to paraphrase Zen. There is truly no way out of that ... because the one who wants out is a phantom!! That "one" ... the "person..." is merely an idea appearing in mind and believed in as a real separate entity. When this is challenged (IF it is challenged, big IF there) then it may be seen through as the emperor who has no clothes. What it seems to take in some instances, many instances, is the questioning and challenging of ALL believed-in identification with anything at all. The Self is NON-Conceptual Aliveness-Wakefulness, Immediate Naked Awareness Presencing and appearing AS all that seemingly IS in this Dream-Play of Consciousness!

This can happen as the unfolding of a natural loving self-examination, an innate curiosity to find out, “what makes 'me' suffer this way?” But there is no “one size fits all." In true non-dual spirituality the path is made by the Inner Guru, which can be conceived by the mind as a Naked Presence or Unadorned Awareness. As Nisargadatta pointed out any “outer guru” or teaching is merely a reflection of that One-Without-a-Second, Presence-Awareness ItSelf, which is the True Guru. That Self-Aware Essence takes the seeker through the false and when that seeming process is complete, there is the Eternal Reality, as It always was, shining in plain sight as that Naked Awareness … just That and nothing else.

But THIS “Nothing” is not the void or “dark night” of the existentialists’ resignation and despair! That Awakeness, Awareness, is a thriving, energetic, motionlessness-moving-aliveness that powers all that appears in this dream of separate beings and ultimately shows that separateness itself to be absolutely insubstantial.

This nothing IS Everything. Nothing/Everything ... This Is "Advaita"" NOT TWO. Or "Dzogchen:" The Great Perfection ...NON-Conceptual Naked Presence. To paraphrase Sri Nisargadatta Maharaj: When it is seen there is nothing, that is wisdom. When it is seen there is everything, that is love. And Life moves between these (apparent) two. In short, THIS Emptiness is FULL with the aliveness of Unconditioned Accepting of all that appears ... THAT ... THIS! ... is a loving embracing Nothing that appears AS everything. Again: NOT TWO.

This is impossible for mind to grasp, as mind IS the idea of “I” as apart from “other-than-I” and therefore merely another of the endless array of insubstantial "objects-in-a-mirror" that arise in Wakeful Awareness.

That Awareness IS what was sought, and along the way if there is despair, then that is what appears as a seeming obscuration to the infinite Isness of your own Being. But these are merely as clouds and storms in the Empty Sky. Appearances, imagination, scenes showing up in the mirror, insubstantial, temporal. No problem at all with any of that unless “you” are there to "think about it.”

My friend goes on to say, "*We are entertaining ourselves to death and missing it all. What we are missing when Zen, with its gift for understatement, tell us, "just this," is this very alive now when all the concern for "me" mysteriously falls away and we struck by the very wonder of it all."*

That is a very lovely way to express The Wonder of Naked Presence arising as all that IS in the appearing-world. Then finally as the search is ended and it is clear that there is no separate "me" or “we” and only This Wonder, Oneness' game of hide-and-seek has ended and here is Life, being lived full on, with endless passion and peace. Allee Allee In Free!

78. Loving To Be No-One

J.S. Writes, *I've got nothing but love for you, Charlie. Tonight has kind of made me reflect on our friendship that's developed over the past few years and tears well up in my eyes. To be alive and to experience/recognize absolute selfless love is a gift. Our friendship has been/is a gift. Have a wonderful now.*

Just absolutely loving to be. No one.

ROGER THAT! Gracias!

All there is, is Love

As there is only NOTHNG, that is wisdom; and, there is only EVERYTHING, that is LOVE".

- *Paraphrasing Sri Nisargadatta*

Appendix One: About The Author

Who Is Talking Here?

Charlie Hayes (14 Dec 1936 -) was born to a prominent family in Washington DC, and grew up to be an eighth grade dropout, a drug-doing and booze-abusing jazz musician, then a married-but-divorced father, racing driver and later a hugely successful Ferrari new and used car dealer with a loving wife and a second (totally charming) son.

Charlie was once named one of the top ten race car drivers in the world, but his career ended in a 160 MPH crash in 1968. Following that Hayes started drinking and doing drugs again (he had stopped for the racing but that was over so it was back to the escape in booze, pot and uppers.)

Following a devastating loss of his business, his marriage and all his possessions in June of 1974, due to the drug and alcohol abuse, Hayes then became a "spiritual seeker. This search went on – taking a variety of forms -- for over three decades. He was first a student of Ramana Maharshi (via books) and attended a "satsang" with Swami Muktananda (whom he would meet again later) in December 1974. He saw the Maharishi Mahesh Yogi on TV in 1975 and was struck by his happy presence, and so he learned "TM" and practiced it diligently.

In 1978 he completed the 'est' training and then worked with est founder Werner Erhard for several months. Then in March 1979 he received "Shaktipat Diksha" initiation from Erhard's close friend, the Indian Guru Swami (Baba) Muktananda, whom he had first met in 1974.

Subsequently he studied Kashmir Shaivism and other eastern scriptures with Muktananda and his successor, Gurumayi Chidvilasananda, for twenty years, and lived in their ashram for two of those years. There was meditation, seva (service) and chanting, and eventually the addictions to drugs and alcohol faded, and there was more peace and gradually improving health ... physical, mental and spiritual.

Early in the new millennium Charlie became a Reiki Master Teacher in the Usui Lineage and began the practice of that discipline. Shortly afterwards met the well-known Indian Guru Sri Sri Ravi Shankar (who had also been a disciple of the Maharishi), in whose presence he experienced a complete realization of the Oneness of all things. However this experience, as is the case with ALL "experiences," went away after a few weeks, and there was "much weeping and wailing and gnashing of teeth."

It had not yet become clear that any experience is impermanent and ONLY that Naked Nondual Awareness is what NEVER changes. In the despair, the understanding was just beginning to dawn, that nothing that changes can be "Real."

In August 2002 Hayes met his first "uncompromising Nonduality" teacher, Wayne Liquorman, and attended numerous Talks, and two long retreats, with him. At this time the book "I Am That," Talks with Sri Nisargadatta Maharaj, came into Charlie's life. He devoured it with great enthusiasm!

When a disagreement with Wayne arose, that then led to meetings with the British Nonduality author of "The Open Secret," Tony Parsons, by telephone. Suffering from deep depression, Charlie also began a practice called "Ishayas' Ascension," a form of meditative Self Inquiry; he continued occasional practice of Transcendental Meditation and "The TM Sidhi Programme" as well.

These helped alleviate the pain but did not lead to "Oneness." No more than drugs and booze had!

Then in late 2004, in what Hayes considers to be the "pivotal occurrence in all this," he met American Nonduality writer John

Wheeler (author of "Awakening To The Natural State" and several other books). The clarity and compassion expressed by Wheeler "lit me up!", he recalls. (John Wheeler is an expression of Advaita Nonduality in the Navnath Sampradaya "lineage" of Sri Nisargadatta Maharaj.)

Subsequently, Charlie traveled to Australia to meet John's mentor, 'Sailor' Bob Adamson, whose own search had ended in the presence of Sri Nisargadatta Maharaj himself.

After that there were further talks with Tony Parsons, Bob Adamson and John Wheeler, and discussions with other "nonduality friends" … notably, Unmani Liza Hyde (author of "I Am Life Itself"), Annette Nibley, and John Wheeler "Graduate" John Greven (author of "Oneness, the Destination you never left.")

Ultimately, All questions and doubts simply dissolved.

Hayes retired from the automobile business and moved to Enid, Oklahoma in June of 2007, and hosts Talks on "Self-Liberation" in Enid and other locations where he is invited to share the Nondual Understanding of what is real, and what is not. He also offers Reiki when asked, and occasionally consults Motorsports teams and drivers who need advice on finding sponsorship for their racing programs.

Now remember, this is ONLY a story. No story is the actual; only a representation of an imaginary life. So don't believe a word of what is said; use what is said to see through your own story to what is unchanging and real.

Appendix Two: Books and Websites

Recommended Books

There are hundreds of great pointer-boos but I have limited this list to the ones I consider to be essentially pure and uncompromising. No "spiritual lollipops" or "Outrageous Myths" will be found in this very short list. This is not in any particular order.

"I Am That" - Talks with Sri Nisargadatta Maharaj

"Oneness, The Destination You Never Left" by John Greven. Get it at www.onenessjustthat.com.

"I Am Unborn" Further Talks with Sri Nisargadatta, available free to download at http://stores.lulu.com/charliehayes36

"You Were Never Born" and other books by John Wheeler, available on Amazon and at www.non-dualitybooks.com

"Nothing Being Everything" and other books by Tony Parsons. Also excellent CDs and DVDs. Get at www.theopensecret.com.

"What's Wrong With Right Now (Unless You Think About It) by 'Sailor' Bob Adamson ... get it on Amazon

"The Outrageous Myths Of Enlightenment" and other books and CDs by Stephen Wingate. Get them at Stephen's Website, at http://www.atmapublishing.com/

"Awakening To The Dream" by Leo Hartong. Get it from Amazon or www.non-dualitybooks.com.

There are a few more, listed on the "Purchases" page, on http://charliehayes36.tripod.com/purchases.html

Recommended Websites:

John Wheeler ... The Natural State
http://www.thenaturalstate.org/

"Sailor" Bob Adamson ... Non-Conceptual Awareness
http://members.iinet.net.au/~adamson7

Tony Parsons ... The Open Secret
http://www.theopensecret.com/

John Greven ... Oneness Just That
http://www.onenessjustthat.com/

Annette Nibley ... What Never Changes
http://www.whatneverchanges.com/

Jeff Foster ... Life Without A Centre
http://www.lifewithoutacentre.com/

Nathan Gill ... Being, The Bottom Line
http://www.nathangill.com/

Leo Hartong ... Awakening To The Dream
http://www.awakeningtothedream.com/

Joan Tollifson ... What Is Real?
http://www.joantollifson.com/

John Astin ... Out Beyond Ideas
http://www.integrativearts.com/blog/

Stephen Wingate ... Living In Peace
http://livinginpeace-thenaturalstate.com/index.html

Chad Barber ... Luminous Living Reality
http://www.strangeflesh.net/index.html

Randall Friend ... You Are Dreaming
http://avastu0.blogspot.com/

Mike Smith ... Instant Truth
http://instanttruth.zaadz.com/blog

Gilbert Schultz ... Nonduality Notes
http://nondualitynotes.blogspot.com/

Unmani (Liza) Hyde ... I Am life Itself
http://www.not-knowing.com/

David Brockman ... The Wonder Of This
http://www.thewonderofthis.com/

Atma Publishing ... Advaita Books & CDs
http://www.atmapublishing.com/

Quotes from Sri Nisargadatta
http://www.mpeters.de/nisargadatta/index.cfm

Sri Nisargadatta Maharaj ... A Beautiful Tribute Website
http://www.nisargadatta.in/WebCMS/CMSPage.aspx?PageID=1

Sri Nisargadatta Maharaj ... "official" Web Site
http://www.nisargadatta.net/

Sri Ramana Maharshi ... "official" Web Site
http://www.ramana-maharshi.org/

"The right disciple will always find the right teacher."- *Sri Nisargadatta Maharaj*

"That in which all these worlds seem to exist steadily, that of which all these worlds are a possession, that from which all these worlds arise, that for which all these exist, that by which all these worlds come into existence and that which is indeed all these - that alone is the existing reality.
Let us cherish that Self, which is the Reality, in the Heart."

- Sri Ramana Maharshi

Consultations, Conference Calls & Meetings

Your comments, questions, insights are most welcome...
e-mail: charliehayes36@yahoo.com, or phone:

Oklahoma, USA + 1-580-366-4083

Visit www.theeternalstate.org

Questions are answered by e-mail whenever possible. Please write your questions and concerns to: non.duality@yahoo.com.

Meetings happen in Enid, Oklahoma on a regular basis. Check the website for a current schedule. Enid is about a 90 minute drive from either Oklahoma City or Tulsa.

You may also join in by Free Telephone Conference Call. See website for details.

30 to 60 minute "One To One" consultations are also available. Those who have participated in these have found them to be very helpful in clarifying the pointers and ending confusion, leaving clarity and increasing freedom from suffering.

To arrange a consultation, write to charliehayes36@yahoo.com with or call USA (Oklahoma) 1-580-366-4083 for available times and other details. Chances are we can call you at no cost to us or you, if you are in the UK, USA, Canada or Mexico.

Charlie is also available to travel to meet with your group. Call for details.

Coda To The Riff:This Is Utterly Paradoxical.

There is in the Ultimate Nondual Is, NO "person" to suffer, to practice, to be therapized, to meditate, to self-enquire, to seek solace and release from pain, to find God, to awaken, to become enlightened, to realize the Self, to attain liberation. Yet "one believes".... ignorantly! ... "I am me." And that belief can (perhaps must!) be investigated, yet there is no-one to "do" that. PARADOX!

There is no separate individual anywhere anywhen to be born, to live, to die, to be resurrected, to incarnate, to re-incarnate. As the Sages have pointed out since the movie show we call "time" began to appear and move on the empty screen of Being, there is no creation, no dissolution, no path, no goal, no seeker, nothing to seek, no truth, no false, no bondage, no liberation. There is nothing. ONLY nothing. This happening of "everything is no more substantial and no more "real" than that movie on the TV screen. Pull the plug on the TV and where did the movie go? Where does the movie come from? Without the energy of "electricity, no movie, so the movie on the TV is actually nothing but an appearance or waves of electricity, shaping and patterning as images and movement. The same with this appearance; the Energy (Shakti) of The IS appears as the creation yet is nothing but energy patterning like a mirage.

Yet the appearance of "me" can be looked into, yet there is no-one to do that. PARADOX!

There is no person, AND the person can investigate itself: Am I a person? What is this "I" called "me?" Where is that I? What is its real nature? There is no-one yet "the individual" ("mind-appearance") must find that for itself. Then there is the seeing that all there is, is nothing… seen by no-one. PARADOX!

You are The Absolute,
Prior To Consciousness,
Prior to Creation,
Prior to Nothing,
Prior to Everything.

That Self arises as
Nothing Being Everything.

Don't refuse to be what you are.
Stop pretending to be what you are not.

Be As You Are

From Love To Love With Love

www.ingramcontent.com/pod-product-compliance
Lightning Source LLC
LaVergne TN
LVHW090935080826
845145LV00003B/755

* 9 7 8 0 9 7 6 6 6 1 9 9 3 *